DISCUSSION PAPER 57

SPONTANEOUS OR PREMEDITATED?
Post-Election Violence in Kenya

GODWIN R. MURUNGA

NORDISKA AFRIKAINSTITUTET, UPPSALA 2011

Indexing terms:
Elections
Violence
Political violence
Political crisis
Ethnicity
Democratization
Kenya

Language checking: Peter Colenbrander

ISSN 1104-8417

ISBN 978-91-7106-694-7

© The author and Nordiska Afrikainstitutet 2011

Production: Byrå4

Print on demand, Lightning Source UK Ltd.

Contents

Foreword

This Discussion Paper is based on a critical examination of the unprecedented levels of political violence that occurred in the aftermath of the Kenyan general elections in 2007. It focuses on post-election violence in Kenya by primarily addressing the roots, complex dynamics and ramifications of political violence in the country and its implications for governance, nation-building and democratisation. The paper analyses two critical issues: the ways in which the lack of consensus among competing factions of the political elite provided the context for violence, and the complicity of some international actors and powers in the outbreak of violence.

Although the fundamental issue is framed around the question of whether post-election violence in Kenya's case was planned or spontaneous, the author carefully transcends this binary, drawing upon Kenya's history, its weak institutions, the nature of its ethnically fractured political elite and political parties, and the complicity of international actors. It also explores in great detail the interface between planned and unplanned violence in the post-election period.

The paper also interrogates the various explanations of post-election violence in Kenya as being impelled by: protests against electoral rigging and the use of state power to perpetrate electoral fraud; politicised inter-ethnic conflict between the Party of National Unity and Orange Democratic Movement supporters; and orchestrated acts of revenge between the opposing sides to the conflict. Also important is the analysis of the political geography of post-electoral violence in Kenya as reflected in the patterns, intensity and spread of the violence and its consequences. The nature and pattern of the violence, including state-sanctioned violence involving the use of the police by the ruling party, are carefully unpacked to unravel the spatial dimensions of planned and unplanned violent political behaviour.

In conclusion, the paper demonstrates how fractures within Kenyan society – a divided political elite and an alienated and angry populace, in a context marked by weak political institutions and the ethnicisation of political parties by an elite locked in a grim struggle for power-at-any cost – plunged the country into unprecedented levels of violence that only ended with the reaching of a political pact between factions of the feuding elite with the aid of regional and international mediators. As such, it goes beyond simplistic explanations of political violence in Africa, and will be of interest to scholars, policymakers and civil society activists seeking a better understanding of the complex challenges facing democratisation, development, peace and security in Kenya.

Cyril Obi
Senior Researcher
The Nordic Africa Institute

'[President] Kibaki is aware that it is bad manners for a sitting President to lose [an election].'

Prof. Macharia Munene, USIU, Nairobi, *East African Standard*, 12 July 2007

An electoral process is an alternative to violence as it is a means of achieving governance. It is when an electoral process is perceived as unfair, unresponsive, or corrupt, that its political legitimacy is compromised and stakeholders are motivated to go outside the established norms to achieve their objectives. Electoral conflict and violence become tactics [of equal importance] in political competition.[1]

---

1. Jeff Fischer, *Electoral Conflict and Violence: A Strategy for Study and Prevention*, IFES White Paper, 2002-01, 5 February 2002, p. 2.

Introduction

Most Kenyans invested their faith in the electoral process prior to the 2007 general elections. They not only expected a transparent process and fair outcome, but also assumed the incumbent would, at the very least, respect their choice. Of course, there were some, like Macharia Munene, who held that it is 'bad manners' for an incumbent president to lose an election, but the majority understood that change or continuity in governance would be decided through the ballot box. They registered to vote in record numbers, braved long voting queues, the hot sun or rainy conditions, and cast their votes in a relatively peaceful process. In spite of the flaws identified by the Kriegler Commission,[2] voting was smooth in most parts of the country, with isolated reports of the tension common to such contests. Trouble started after voting. It was centred on the national tallying centre at the Kenyatta International Conference Centre (KICC) in Nairobi.

This paper attempts to provide some explanations of the nature of the electoral troubles and the subsequent crisis that brought Kenya to near collapse, leading to the deaths of at least 1,133 people and the displacement of over 350,000.[3] The paper is of the view that Kenya's electoral violence was a consequence of the abuse of the electoral process, even though we acknowledge this abuse and subsequent violence was linked to longer-term historical grievances that had been simmering in the country.

The paper identifies and maps the main forms of violence, seeking thereby to analyse their manifestations in different regions and provide preliminary explanations for any divergences between regions. It concludes with a brief discussion of the debates on peace, truth and justice. The analysis illustrates the inconsistency of the political class in Kenya in relation to political violence. It is notable that on the critical issue of punishment of those who organised and funded violence, erstwhile political protagonists have found common ground in opposing punishment and consequently denied justice to those who were killed, displaced or whose property was destroyed. It is on this basis that the issue of impunity runs through election politics and remains at the centre of discussions of election violence in Kenya.

This paper posits a relationship between abuse of electoral processes and the

---

2. Refers to the Independent Review Commission (IREC) on the general elections that was chaired by a former South African appeal court judge, Johann Kriegler, whose report is variously referred to in this paper as IREC or Kriegler Report. See Note 3.

3. These are the figures reported by the Republic of Kenya, *Report of the Commission of Inquiry into Post Election Violence (CIPEV)*, Nairobi: Government Printers, 2008. See pp. 346 and 352 (hereafter referred to as CIPEV Report). Depending on the sources used, the numbers will differ but the CIPEV Report has the advantage of being based on a comprehensive review of the violence.

eruption of election-related violence. It underscores the view in the epigraph that an 'electoral process is an alternative to violence as it is a means of achieving governance.' When an electoral process is manipulated and abused, the legitimacy of the governance outcome is questionable and the premium placed on choice undermined. Choice matters in an electoral process. Abuse of the electoral system and process necessarily invites alternative means of achieving legitimate government. It is in this sense that the paper conceptualises (street) protests as a legitimate form of political expression. With specific reference to post-election Kenya, protests became a means of achieving governance where the ballot box failed.

Like the ballot box, street protests are susceptible to manipulation and abuse. But such abuse happens, in part, because the legitimacy of government as guardian of fair and just choice is compromised. Unlike the ballot box, though, streets are not easy to discipline. Rather, protests carry with them all the baggage that is not visible in the simple act of casting a ballot. This baggage can very easily lead to events that spiral out of control. In post-election Kenya, protest and violence were conjoined in a spiral that shifted from its initial noble intention of challenging the illegitimate installation of Kibaki to out-of-control murderousness. This escalation consequently exposed the inability of government to take charge and of the political class to control its constituencies. Post-election violence (PEV) therefore reflected mounting instability in Kenya.

Post-Election Violence: Overview of the Literature

Three main forms of violence occurred in post-election Kenya. These were spontaneous, premeditated or planned and state-directed. All are connected in one way or other to historical injustices relating to land, human rights abuse and the political class's obstinate refusal to institute long-overdue and wide-ranging political reforms. We categorise them here largely for conceptual reasons since, in their daily occurrence, no Chinese wall neatly separates different forms of violence or separates them from their contexts. In fact, these forms overlapped, reinforced or undermined each other in a complicated relationship. But above all, the halting project of democratisation in Kenya provides a context for understanding their occurrence.

This is not the first study of PEV in Kenya. Available analyses have examined violence as a catastrophic consequence of impunity within the ruling class and the state; as due to the 'normalisation of violence' in society and also as a consequence of weak institutions that have been repeatedly abused. These are in one way or other then related to abuse of electoral processes and procedure which, for many, was the final trigger for the violent explosion.[4]

The theme of weak institutions recurs in the literature. Institutions are often portrayed as captured by the local ruling class who put them to politically expedient uses. Here, Kenya's political class is characterised as 'beholden to political myopia and moral bankruptcy' and lacks the will to 'imagine a larger national interest' beyond its own.[5] As such, members of the class use their control of and protection by the state not only to manipulate institutions of governance in their favour, but also to act in complete disregard of the law and due processes, knowing the very limited consequences that can result for them and their political careers. Their hesitancy to institute radical reforms is related to their ability to mobilise politics from above mostly through the ethnic prism. As illustration, analysts point to Kibaki's unilateral appointment of 16 new Electoral Commission of Kenya (ECK) commissioners just months before the elections in disregard of the interparty parliamentary group agreement of 1997 that sanctioned consultation prior to such appointments.[6]

In turn, mobilising from above has been a catalyst for acrimony rather than harmony in Kenya. Leaders not only undermined nation-building by sowing discord among citizens, but also pitted communities against each other in the struggles for political supremacy and the economic rewards that go with high office. The state is the ultimate prize, as access to it guarantees economic gain. Through the state, politicians are guaranteed a level of control over resources and popular forces, either through coercion or acquiescence. This control has been decisive in keeping politicians in power irrespective of their contribution to the national project. Makau Mutua proposes civil society as 'the only sector that can fundamentally renew the political class' and lead the reform process, but the worth of this recommendation is limited. Like the state, civil society has its weaknesses, including reported cases of internal fragmentation and lack of probity. Indeed, political myopia and moral bankruptcy are not foreign to civil society. Furthermore, the progressive element within civil society has very weak

---

4. See the CIPEV Report; IREC, *Report of the Independent Review Commission on the General Elections* held in Kenya on the 27 December 2007, Nairobi: Government Printers, 2008; International Crisis Group, *Kenya in Crisis*, Africa Report no. 137, 21 February 2008; KNCHR, *On the Brink of the Precipice: A Human Rights Account of Kenya's Post-2007 Election Violence*, Nairobi: KNCHR, 2008; Susanne Mueller, 'The Political Economy of Kenya's Crisis,' in *Journal of Eastern African Studies (JEAS)*, vol. 2, no.2, 2008; essays in *Journal of Contemporary African Studies*, vol. 27, no. 3, 2009; and essays in Jérôme Lafargue, ed. *The General Elections in Kenya, 2007*, Dar es Salaam: Mkuki na Nyota, 2009.

5. Makau Mutua, *Kenya's Quest for Democracy: Taming Leviathan*, Boulder and London: Lynne Rienner, 2009, p. 3.

6. See Bård A. Andreassen, et. al., '"I Acted Under a Lot of Pressure": The Disputed 2007 Kenyan General Election in Context,' *NORDEM Report*, 7/2008, chap. II.

links to popular forces in society, a fact made worse by the much talked-about 'paradigm paralysis' in civil society following the end of the Moi/KANU rule[7]

The prevalence of violence in society is connected, in Susanne Mueller's view, to the character of the elite in power and the weak institutions of law enforcement, among others. Mueller writes of the diffusion of violence in society, which, together with the deliberate undermining of institutions of governance and the ethnicisation of political parties, rendered the governance system vulnerable.[8] Political violence has consequently been treated as an integral and normalised element which, according to Anderson and Lochery, 'Kenyans have learned to live with' as 'part of politics.'[9] The political class encourages non-state actors to take violent action, since they 'depend on violence to build electoral influence.' In turn, they limit the ability of the state to govern effectively and their choice has included lining up militia groups whose creation, financing and deployment they control or in some way facilitate.

Several studies track the rise, transformation and impacts of militia groups. It is clear that land dispossession resulting from the ethnic clashes of the 1992 and 1997 elections, urban decay that took root around this period and the general proliferation of illicit activities in rural and urban settings all contribute to the visibility of and give 'voice' to these groups. Peter Kagwanja and David Anderson ably show how the religio-cultural Mungiki grouping was transformed into a criminal and vigilante gang terrorising and murdering people and, where possible, forcibly extracting rent.[10] While agreeing with this description, other

---

7. For a critique of civil society in Kenya, see Shadrack W. Nasong'o, 'Negotiating New Rules of the Game: Social Movements, Civil Society and the Kenyan Transition,' in Godwin R. Murunga and Shadrack W. Nasong'o, (eds), *Kenya: Struggles for Democracy*, London and Dakar: Zed Books in Association with CODESRIA, 2007, pp. 19-57; Nasong'o, *The Human Rights Sector in Kenya: Key Issues and Challenges*, Occasional Paper No. 2, 2009 and Mutahi Ngunyi, 'Civil Society in the Post-Amendment Context,' A Consultant's Report to the Royal Norwegian Embassy, Nairobi Kenya, June 2008. By 'paradigm paralysis,' Ngunyi refers to the fact that civil society was organised as a bulwark against the Moi/KANU regime, a basis of organisation and unity that was withdrawn once Moi retired and KANU lost power in 2002.

8. See Susanne Mueller, 'The Political Economy of Kenya's Crisis'; Lynch, 'Courting the Kalenjin: The Failure of Dynasticism and the Strength of the ODM Wave in the Kenya's Rift Valley Province,' in *African Affairs*, vol. 107, no. 429, 2008, p. 567. For a study that illustrates how institutions that safeguard property rights in land have been strengthened or deliberately weakened in Kenya, see Ato Kwamena Onoma, *The Politics of Property Rights Institutions in Africa*, Cambridge: Cambridge University Press, 2010.

9. David Anderson and Emma Lochery, 'Violence and Exodus in Kenya's Rift Valley, 2008: Predictable and Preventable?' in *JEAS*, vol. 2, no. 2, 2008, p. 338.

10. See Grace N. Wamue, 'Revisiting Our Indigenous Shrines through Mungiki,' in *African Affairs*, vol. 100, no.400, 2001, pp. 453-67 ; Peter Kagwanja, 'Facing Mount Kenya or Facing Mecca? The Mungiki, Ethnic Violence and the Politics of the Moi Succession in Kenya, 1987–2002,' in *African Affairs*, vol. 102, no. 406, 2003, pp. 25-49; David Anderson, 'Vigilantes, Violence and the Politics of Public Order in Kenya,' in *African Affairs*, vol. 101, no.405, 2002, pp. 531–55.

analysts like Katumanga broaden the argument by showing that militia groups are central to what is described as Kenya's 'bandit economy,' which has much to do with the upper as well as lower classes.[11] According to these studies, petty crime, vigilantism and elite politics do not operate in isolation but are linked to the broader 'instrumentalisation of disorder' in Kenya.[12] These studies, however, seem to celebrate or at least fail to critique the assumption, common to some conceptual studies, that 'Africa works' through disorder. As such, they ignore evidence of civic protest against predatory systems, evidence that strongly suggests Kenyans neither celebrate nor want disorder.

Rarely discussed is the issue of state capacity both in its historical and contemporary sense in order to contextualise the proliferation of violent crime and seeming disorder. 'Disorder' has a history that is often missed in the studies of militia and vigilante groups. The ability to exercise effective governance and sustain a democratic culture is influenced by the historical weaknesses of the state and other incapacities fostered in the era of neoliberal adjustment programmes. These reforms called for rolling back the state to free the private sector. However, the weaknesses of the local private sector and the fact that this sector cannot effectively step in to take care of most social service functions was hardly acknowledged.[13]

Adjustment programmes embodied the twin objective of economic reforms and political liberalisation. The latter was framed as opening political space for competitive multi-party politics. Lacking in any detailed contextual appreciation of local politics, democratisation was defined largely in terms of periodic competitive elections. Multi-party elections have thus occupied a central place in Africa's second *uhuru*. But the process has been challenged and undermined by weaknesses in internal political cultures in Africa, especially by incumbents who often are insecure and scared of real electoral competition. Incumbent dictatorships have remained stubbornly resilient in the face of greater popular

11. See Musambayi Katumanga, 'A City under Siege: Banditry and Modes of Accumulation in Nairobi, 1991-2004,' *Review of African Political Economy*, no. 106, 2005, pp. 505–20.

12. The broad outline of the 'instrumentalisation of disorder' and 'retraditionalisation of society' are found in Patrick Chabal and Jean-Pascal Daloz, *Africa Works. The Political Instrumentalization of Disorder*, Bloomington IN: International African Institute in association with James Currey and Indiana University Press, 1999 and Stephen Ellis, *The Mask of Anarchy: The Destruction of Liberia and the Religious Dimension of an African Civil War*, London: Hurst 1999. They are applied to the Kenyan case by Peter M. Kagwanja, '"Power to Uhuru": Youth Identity and Generational Politics in Kenya's 2002 Elections,' *Africa Affairs*, vol. 105, no. 418, 2006, pp. 51–75.

13. See generally Adebayo Olukoshi, *The Elusive Prince of Denmark: Structural Adjustment and the Crisis of Governance in Africa*, NAI Research Report Series, no. 104, 1998; Thandika Mkandawire and Charles C. Soludo, *Our Future, our Continent: African Perspectives on Structural Adjustment*, Ottawa and Dakar: IDRC and CODESRIA, 1999. For Kenya, see Murunga, 'Governance and the Politics of Structural Adjustment in Kenya,' in Murunga and Nasong'o, (eds), *Kenya: Struggles for Democracy*, pp. 263–300.

pressures. In the process, the need for citizens to exercise meaningful choice in elections has been ignored, constricted or never really given a chance, as many either vote without choosing, or their votes simply do not count. Africa's non-transition has therefore been characterised by civilianised military regimes and 'elected' dictators that render competitive electoral processes a facade.[14]

There are some gains in the opening up of political space and the institution-alisation, codification and entrenching of basic rights and freedoms, including freedoms of speech and assembly.[15] But the promise of the third wave of democ-ratisation in Africa has hardly been met with respect to the livelihood needs of the majority. Poverty, illiteracy and disease dot the environment and in many cases have worsened since the adjustment era. Life remains an all-consuming struggle for basic survival. Landlessness has increased, as land ownership is sub-jected to a land-reform process informed by neoliberal free market logic.[16]

On the other hand, unemployment has skyrocketed with retrenchment, job cuts and hiring freezes. All these, coupled with a youth bulge, combine to make the struggle for democracy not only a context for resistance to imposed forms of liberal democracy but also a potent opportunity for reprisal against an ill-conceived multi-party system that is 'prising the people out of politics.' These are consuming struggles for survival: they leave little room for the exercise of meaningful electoral choice. Worse, the options on offer represent 'a tyranny of choice(s)' in which, to use Cyril Obi's argument, the 'people are confronted with a particular type of democracy that they do not fully understand or relate to' and in which they constantly see betrayal by the political class.[17] Liberal democ-

14. Said Adejumobi, 'Elections in Africa: A Fading Shadow of Democracy,' in *International Political Science Review*, vol. 21, no. 1, 2000, pp. 59–73; Julius Ihonvbere, 'Where is the Third Wave? A Critical Evaluation of Africa's Non-Transition to Democracy,' in *Africa Today*, vol. 43, no. 4, 1996, pp. 343–67.

15. On these gains, see Adebayo Olukoshi, 'Changing Patterns of Politics in Africa,' in Atilio A. Boron and Gladys Lechini, (eds), *Politics and Social Movements in an Hegemonic World: Lessons from Africa, Asia and Latin America*, Buenos Aires: CLACSO, 2005; Abdul Raufu Mustapha and Lindsay Whitfield, *Turning Points in African Democracy*, London: James Currey, 2009.

16. For a description of the contours of this logic, see Ambreena Manji, *The Politics of Land Reform in Africa: From Communal Tenure to Free Market*, London: Zed Books, 2006 and Issa G. Shivji (edited by Godwin R. Murunga) *Where is Uhuru? Reflections on the Struggle for Democracy in Africa*, Oxford: FAHAMU Books, 2009, chapters 9 and10.

17. Claude Ake, *Democracy and Development in Africa*, Washington DC: The Brookings Institution, 1996; Cyril I. Obi, *No Choice, But Democracy: Prising the People Out of Politics in Africa?* Claude Ake Memorial Paper No. 2, Department of Peace and Conflict Research, Uppsala University and Nordic Africa Institute, 2008, p. 9.

racy, in the sense of this tyranny, is not an empowering experience but, as Fantu Cheru shows, an ideology of domination.[18]

By far the weakest link in the never-ending drama of democratisation is the area of social justice. Elections as presently constituted have failed to address social policy and welfare issues. Instead, such issues are treated as a part of belt-tightening measures. Improvements to 'popular livelihoods' are left outside the expected gains from this democratisation process, as if they are supposed to accrue naturally from democracy. This further limits possibilities of choice in an election by facilitating alienation of the poor from governance. In other words, elections are not really sites of making choices in the strict sense of installing popular power. Where a semblance of competition is kept, choice is circumscribed by the elite struggle over raw power and the choicelessness that this represents. Elections must be credible to be accepted: they must provide a genuine choice if they are to count and count equally.

However, the legitimacy of violent protests even in this context remains a matter of debate. How does one analyse the Kenyan PEV to underscore the legitimacy of street protests without violating the memory of victims? We argue that the violence was an inevitable part of the struggle for reform which, lacking the requisite organisational discipline of the ballot box, was abused to murderous ends. In Kenya, this occurred as an attempt to delegitimise the flawed Kibaki mandate.

A Note on the Kenyan Democratisation Processes

Kenya's progress towards democratic consolidation since the early 1990s has been slow and halting. Even after the first multi-party elections in 1992, the Moi/KANU regime remained stubbornly authoritarian. Moi continued to limit civic liberties and to manipulate economic policies for political expediency. Under external pressure, he implemented austerity measures that increased poverty and heightened inequalities. He also entrenched ethnic and factional suspicions, and buttressed old hatreds while fanning new conflicts. The 1992 and 1997 ethnic clashes occurred under his watch. They marked a turning point in Kenya's electoral politics, with most subsequent ethnic violence occurring around election time. Many hoped that his retirement and Kibaki's assumption of power in 2002 would lead to a return to respect for basic liberties, enhance transpar-

---

18. See part I of Shivji, *Where is Uhuru?*; Fantu Cheru, 'The Silent Revolution and the Weapons of the Weak: Transformation and Innovation from Below,' in S. Gill and Jim Mittelman (eds), *Innovation and Transformation in International Studies,* Cambridge: Cambridge University Press, 1997.

ency and growth of benefit to Kenyans. But this did not happen and Kibaki's achievements in the first term fell far short of popular expectations.[19]

In the last days of KANU rule, Kenyans were at an all time low in terms of what they expected from the leadership. Moi's abysmal performance was responsible for this. The economy almost ground to a halt, corruption and malfeasance escalated, the infrastructure fell into dilapidation and agriculture slumped. Kibaki was therefore not simply expected to perform better than Moi on key governance and economic indicators – he easily surpassed this task in the first few years of his presidency. The expectation was that Kibaki would consolidate the gains and usher in a new era of prosperity in the country. Thus, Kenyans expected a regime that would deal with the fundamentals of resuscitating the economy and ensuring sustained growth. They also expected equitable redistribution of resources and proportionate allocation in government appointments. These were issues that would begin to address impunity and historical ethnic imbalances that had previously fed into ethnic animosities and undermined democratic consolidation.

The demand for a new constitution and an accompanying truth, justice and reconciliation process clearly indicated how economic growth per se was inadequate to addressing historical grievances. Kenyans vouched for a truth, justice and reconciliation process that would candidly explore historical injustices and heal the resulting pain. They demanded a different governance structure that would decentralise power from the presidency in Nairobi to facilitate a new and inclusive political culture. This new structure would be nested in a new constitutional architecture. Kibaki was unable to adopt as promised a new constitution within the first 100 days of his election campaign. The ensuing debate over constitutional review repeatedly referred to the unfulfilled promises, which touched on equity, justice and fairness both in human rights and social justice, including in the area of gender justice. The desire to prioritise national cohesion by fully engaging the plurality of communities in the country had been embedded in the multi-ethnic vote that catapulted Kibaki to power, a vote that paid

---

19. See Murunga and Nasong'o, 'Bent on Self-Destruction: The Kibaki Regime in Kenya,' in *Journal of Contemporary African Studies*, vol. 24, no. 1, 2006, pp. 1–28; Frank Holmquist, 'Kenya's Antipolitics,' in *Current History*, May 2005, pp. 209–15. There is some consensus that the Kibaki regime has performed much better than the Moi regime on the economic front, but there is also controversy on whether the benefits of this growth have trickled down to a large plurality of Kenyans. See, for instance, Michael Chege, 'Weighed Down by Old Ethnic Baggage: Kenya Races to Another historic Election,' at http://csis.org/blog/weighed-down-old-ethnic-baggage-kenya-races-another-historic-election posted on 22 June 2007 (accessed 19 October 2009).

scant attention to his ethnicity and focused on his 'cosmopolitan image.'[20] But this vote was scattered among regional and ethnic groupings.

Only two years into his leadership, Kibaki and the political class around him undermined hopes of building an inclusive democratic system. A good many of this political class were appointed to key positions in government from where they exuded their arrogance. They included George Muhoho (Kenya Ports Authority), Joe Wanjui (Chancellor of the University of Nairobi), Njenga Karume (Minister for Defence), John Michuki (Minister for Internal Security), Nathaniel Kang'ethe (then Director Kenya Revenue Authority), Eddy Njoroge (KENGEN), Julius Gecau (formerly at Kenya Power and Lighting Company), to name but a few. Not only did their arrogance soar to new heights, but it also regularly clouded their judgment on important national issues. Their collective actions eventually scattered the pre-election alliance that had sent Moi and KANU packing. For instance, the political class instituted new ethno-regional imbalances in political appointments and in resource allocation, leading to many replays of habits identified with the previous discredited regime.

Their actions and arrogance predictably provoked the ire of the coalition partners in the Liberal Democratic Party (LDP) group, which felt cheated. LDP mounted sustained criticism of the 'new' Kibaki. Eventually, to bolster his position *vis-à-vis* an increasingly vocal LDP-wing of the National Rainbow Coalition (NARC), Kibaki appointed to cabinet positions some discredited KANU-era politicians.[21] Furthermore, his allies intensified efforts to frustrate or derail the constitutional review process that had been under way for at least a decade. The popular draft (Bomas Draft) of the constitution that had been crafted through a people-driven and consultative process was abandoned. In its place, an alternative (Wako Draft) was presented to a referendum in November 2005 but was soundly rejected.[22]

The low-point of this self-destructive politics seemed to be the attack on the media. In March 2006, hired goons working in collaboration with police at-

---

20. Stephen N. Ndegwa, 'Kenya: Third Time Lucky?' in *Journal of Democracy*, vol. 14, no. 3, 2003, pp. 145–58; Lucy Oriang writing in the *Daily Nation*, 11 February 2005 noted that Kibaki 'had enough of a cosmopolitan image to appeal to Kenyans across the board' and wondered how 'he and his team have managed to throw it away in just two years.'

21. Kiraitu Murungi and Amos Kimunya epitomised this arrogance in some of their public statements. Kimunya dismissed land title deeds issued under Moi as pieces of paper while Murungi instructed 'Moi to go home, herd goats and watch TV to see how government is run.' See 'Genesis of Rift Valley Rebellion,' in *The Standard*, 30 December 2007. On ethno-regional imbalances, the Society for International Development (SID) Report remains the best evidence so far. See *Readings on Inequality in Kenya: Sectoral Dynamics and Perspectives*, Nairobi: SID, 2006.

22. Jill Cottrell and Yash Ghai, 'Constitution Making and Democratisation in Kenya (2000–2005), in *Democratisation*, vol.14, no.1, 2007, pp.1–25; see also Willy Mutunga, *Constitution Making from the Middle: Civil Society and Transition Politics in Kenya 1992-1997*, Nairobi: SAREAT, 1999.

tacked the Standard Media Group. These Armenian goons had been smuggled into the country by senior security officials against all known protocol. They almost completely disabled the media house's facilities. To add to this insult, the minister of state in charge of internal security, John Michuki, arrogantly and unapologetically retorted that 'When you rattle a snake, be prepared to be bitten.' All along, the Kibaki government continued to tolerate high-level corruption within the cabinet, with close ministers like David Mwiraria and Kiraitu Murungi caught on tape speaking approvingly in relation to the Anglo-Leasing scandal.[23] But it was the blatant announcement of Kibaki as winner of the 2007 election followed by the banning of all live media broadcasts that marked the turning point. This triggered widespread violence that rendered the police ineffective and crippled the country for days in early 2008.

The resulting PEV was a severe test of Kenya's experiment with democratisation. Until then, the country's democratic experiment had been slouching, although the smooth transition from Moi to Kibaki and the defeat of government in the 2005 referendum gave the impression that leadership could accommodate defeat and respect the people's choice. This assumption was widely held in the pre-election period, with some observers even believing the elections were not 'riggable'.

Many viewed Kenya as an island of peace in a turbulent region. After all, indicators and publicly available pre-election calculations made electoral fraud a serious political risk. Indeed, electioneering saw heightened civilian vigilance against rigging, making most pre-balloting fraud extremely difficult, costly and unlikely. The flawed tallying process rudely upset these assumptions and the consequent violence confirmed Jeff Fischer's argument that 'when conflict or violence occurs, it is not a result of an electoral process; it is the breakdown of an electoral process.'[24]

Violence left indelible imprints across the country that expose the tortured road Kenya will likely tread towards democratic consolidation. Violence reached almost every corner of the nation, displacing communities and shaking up local politicians and the international community. Both had been cynical of the mass of voters, and the international community had privately condoned or

---

23. Gladwell Otieno, 'The NARC's Anti-Corruption Drive: Somewhere Over the Rainbow?, in *Africa Security Review*, vol. 14, no. 4, 2005; Michela Wrong, *It's Our Time to Eat: The Story of a Kenyan Whistle Blower*, London: Fourth Estate, 2009.

24. Fischer, *Electoral Conflict and Violence*, p. 2.

supported Kibaki's re-election by every means possible.[25] In the wake of post-election violence, 1,133 people died and close to 350,000 were displaced. The numbers, it must be pointed out, mask the extent of the horror experienced by individual victims on both sides and fail to recognise that this instance was the culmination of extended instability occasioned by the gradual breakdown in law and order and the rise in impunity.

Clash of Interpretations

There are two interpretations of political violence in recent writings. One focuses on the identity of perpetrators and pleads on behalf of victims. This interpretation centres on the morality of violent action. The other insists on PEV as a social protest against a discredited regime whose abuse of the ballot process explains the descent into chaos.

The first interpretation has two voices. One, constituted mostly by Western journalistic reporting, speaks of tribal fights, while the other writes of ethnic cleansing. The *New York Times* reporter Jeffrey Gettlemen, for instance, reported that violence seemed 'to have tapped into an atavistic vein of tribal tension that always lay beneath the surface in Kenya but until now had not produced widespread mayhem.'[26] This is a crude account that eludes the material basis of the violence in its search for a familiar 'darker and bestial' Africa. It misses out the fact that violence is not simply about ethnicity, but that it is the ways in which ethnicities relate to political and economic power that explain the nature and extent of political violence. As Oduor Ong'wen explains elsewhere, 'Kenyans are not polarised because they belong to different ethnic groups. They are divided because they relate differently to the country's natural and productive resources.'[27]

The renowned Kenyan novelist Ngũgĩ wa Thiong'o articulated the ethnic cleansing aspect of the argument. In his intervention, which came hours after the burning of a church at Kiambaa in the Rift Valley which led to the deaths of 17 people, Ngũgĩ lamented the deaths and placed the responsibility on the political opposition, citing politicians in the Rift Valley. Pointing out that 'ethnic cleansing' was taking place in Kenya, Ngũgĩ nevertheless decoupled election

---

25. The *New York Times* cites evidence that the US ambassador favoured Kibaki. According to the Kenneth Flottman, the East African director of the International Republican institute, Ambassador Michael E. Ranneberger tried to influence the perceptions of Kenya by preferring the release of opinion polls that favoured Kibaki and by making public statements that praised Kibaki and minimised Kenyan corruption. See Mike McIntire and Jeffrey Gettleman, 'A Chaotic Kenya Vote and a Secret US Exit Poll,' in *New York Times*, 31 January 2009, p. A1.

26. Gettlemen 'Disputed Vote Plunges Kenya into Bloodshed,' *New York Times*, 31 December 2007.

27. Oduor Ong'wen, 'Class vs. Kinship in Kenya's Eruption to Violence,' in *Wajibu*, vol. 23, no. 1, 2008, p. 17.

rigging from ethnic cleansing, claiming that 'rigged elections is one thing ... but ethnic cleansing is another matter altogether.' He refused to appreciate the connection between the two. When it happened barely a month later that a gang killed 40 people in Naivasha in one day, most of whom were not Gikuyu, Ngũgĩ did not appear similarly angered.[28]

While Ngũgĩ's lament is understandable, it decontextualises Kenyan realities prior to the elections and treats *violence as if it is its own explanation*. For him, all one needs to do is to insert into the narrative 'political instigators' and gullible 'ordinary people' and the rest, it is assumed, makes sense. Ngũgĩ argues that 'ordinary people do not wake up one morning and suddenly decide to kill their neighbours.' They are incited. 'Ethnic cleansing is often instigated by the political elite of one community against another community. It is premeditated, often an order from political warlords.'[29] But do ordinary people simply respond to every incitement without thinking? Ngũgĩ ignores the fact that in the absence of perceived injustice, ordinary people are never that gullible about the machinations of political instigators. In this particular case, and contrary to his earlier work on peasants, Ngũgĩ seems to deny ordinary people the capacity to think.

There is a better analysis that locates the violence in the dangerously deteriorating context obtaining in Kenya prior to elections. These narratives retrace the moment of 'original sin' in Kibaki's first term, when a Gikuyu elite moulded their sense of entitlement to the presidency. This entitlement, together with the arrogance discussed above, precipitated the break-up of NARC and made it impossible to cobble future pre- or post-election elite consensus involving the Gikuyu. Not only did this situation defeat the pre-election alliance of the 2002 elections, the subsequent jockeying among politicians as the 2007 presidential vote neared proceeded on the tacit assumption that one could never make a coalition deal with the Gikuyu elite. Subsequently, this undermined any opportunity for an inter-ethnic alliance that would include the Gikuyu elite.[30]

Those in favour of Gikuyu entitlement to the presidency dug in and sought to consolidate their hold on power. They claimed this almost as a right taken away when Moi took power in 1978. In the victim narrative that they adopted, emphasis was placed on the suffering of the Gikuyu under Moi and the need to secure the presidency in the house of Mumbi, the presumed eponymous founder of the Gikuyu community.

---

28. On Ngugi's reaction, see Ngugi Laments Kenya Violence, http://news.bbc.co.uk/2/hi/africa/7180946.stm (accessed 10 January 2008). See CIPEV Report, pp. 120–1 on the killings.

29. Ngugi Laments Kenya Violence, http://news.bbc.co.uk/2/hi/africa/7180946.stm (accessed 10 January 2008).

30. See Tade Akin Aina, 'The Kenyan Crisis 2007-08 and the Re-Making of an Elite Consensus –Pathways and Pitfalls, 'Lecture Delivered at the Public Forum organized by ARRF and DPMF held on Wednesday, 3 September 2008 at the KICC, Nairobi.

The social protest interpretation is common to those against this Gikuyu entitlement. They accept the view that PEV was due to election rigging, which 'more or less invited popular rebellion against that unpopular and unjust abuse of the people's sovereignty.'[31] But in explaining the social protest, they minimise and at times ignore the horrible violence that took over and overshadowed the protest. Yet this violence was planned as a counter-strategy of taming the Gikuyu elite. This became an all-consuming struggle used to electrify election campaigns and mobilise constituencies. The campaigns became dangerous electoral contests in which hate speech and preferred policy statements almost became indistinguishable. The discourse around *majimbo* was emblematic of this contest, with communities in the Rift Valley interpreting the federalist agenda adopted by the Orange Democratic Movement (ODM) campaign to mean eliminating 'non-native' and therefore 'non-belonging' ethnicities from within their midst.[32] The mass of Gikuyu settlers in the Rift Valley became targets. This began as a mild discourse aimed at fostering 'a sense of Kalenjin *we-ness*.' Like the Gikuyu elite, the Kalenjin also deployed well-known grievances framed in terms of 'state persecution against the Kalenjin' following the retirement of Moi and defeat of KANU.[33] Eventually, this became the basis upon which the exaggerated idea that the election was a contest of 'forty one tribes against one' developed.[34]

From this point onwards, the hateful discourse of eliminating foreigners in 'our' midst matured. In most cases, this referred to people of Gikuyu and Gusii ethnicities, the Gikuyu being reduced simply to the referent of *madoa doa* (spots) in the Rift Valley. There was mutual contempt within the political class, which killed the prospect of any elite consensus to mitigate the hateful discourse as voting day neared. Binyavanga Wainaina writes that 'the most visible Gikuyus said nothing about the rising sense of a Gikuyu establishment' as most opinion leaders took a decidedly partisan stand. Even Kenya's new 'cardinal took, exclusively, his tribe's position in the political debates' thereby eliminating himself

31. See Peter Anyang' Nyong'o, 'Ocampo's Hour of Reckoning is Here, We can't Beat Any Retreat,' *Daily Nation*, 5 November 2009.

32. On the general history and idea of *majimbo*, see David Anderson, '*Majimboism*: The Troubled History of an Idea,' in Daniel Branch, Nic Cheeseman and Leigh Gardner (eds), *Our Turn to Eat: Politics in Kenya Since 1950*, Berlin: LIT Verlag, 2010; see also Mutahi Ngunyi, 'Resuscitating the *Majimbo* Project: The Politics of Deconstructing the Unitary State in Kenya,' in Adebayo O. Olukoshi and Liisa Laakso (eds), *Challenges to the Nation-State in Africa*, Uppsala: Nordic Africa Institute, 1996, pp. 183–213. On the *majimbo* idea in the constitution review process, see Yash Ghai, 'Devolution: Restructuring the Kenyan State,' in *JEAS*, vol. 2. no. 2, 2008, pp. 211-26.

33. Lynch, 'Courting the Kalenjin: The Failure of Dynasticism and the Strength of the ODM Wave in the Kenya's Rift Valley Province,' in *African Affairs*, vol. 107, no. 429, 2008, pp. 556–7.

34. See Michael Chege, 'Kenya: Back From the Brink? in *Journal of Democracy*, vol. 19, no. 4, 2009, p. 132. Chege, like many others who cite this ethnic calculation, ignore the fact that in the Rift Valley the target of violence also included the Gusii community.

from proffering wise counsel in the event of conflict.[35] Ngũgĩ's own endorsement of Kibaki also meant that a regime full of turncoats had won the support of the most progressive writer of our independence history.

The focus on 'political instigators' of criminal violence in itself is inadequate to explaining the different forms of violence. To better illuminate the post-election situation in Kenya, Klopp and Kamungi argue that violence 'needs to be disaggregated and analysed carefully' to 'better understand the various kinds of violence and each side's responsibility.'[36] Are there circumstances that make violence thinkable for instigators and perpetrators? To answer this question and appreciate the interacting roles of genuine protests and gruesome murder and rape, let us start by conceptually contrasting the 'ballot box' and the 'street.'

The Ballot Box and the Street

Kenya has conducted periodic elections since independence in 1963. These are perceived as the basis upon which the people's choice of their leadership is determined. Indeed, in a democratic system at whose core lies party and/or electoral competition, elections are a means of achieving governance, a way to influence the character and content of the leadership and to construct a democratic culture in the country. Yet Kenya is no more democratic simply by virtue of faithfully holding periodic elections. In fact, for a long time Kenya was a *de jure* one-party state and its leadership has often been decided irrespective of actual vote tallies. In other words, elections have not translated into meaningful choice in Kenya. This has contributed to the widespread disenchantment with elections.[37]

For elections to be meaningful, votes must count. Elections cannot simply be periodic rituals devoid of actual choice. In a functioning democracy, the ballot box occupies priority as a site of exercising choice and determining representa-

---

35. See Binyavanga Wainaina, 'In Gikuyu, for Gikuyu, of Gikuyu,' in *Granta* 103, Autumn 2008 http://www.granta.com/Magazine/Granta-103/Letter-From/1. Ngũgĩ wa Thiong'o' had endorsed Kibaki's rule as the 'freest in Kenya's history' in what has been described as the 'Letter of James to the People of Limuru.' The letter entitled 'Protect Your Families: Vote for an MP with Integrity' was written to the people of Limuru dated 23 December 2003. 'Letter of James to the People of Limuru' was the title of Garnette Oluoch-Olunya's Mary Kingsley Zochonis Lecture presented at the ASAUK 2008 held at University of Central Lancashire, Preston, UK from 11–13 September 2008.

36. Jacqueline Klopp and Prisca Kamungi, 'Violence and Elections: Will Kenya Collapse?' in *World Policy Journal*, vol. 24, no. 2, 2007–08, p. 12.

37. Claude Ake wrote of people voting without choosing and characterised this as a process of disempowerment; Thandika Mkandawire called it choice-less democracies. Said Adejumobi describes elections in Africa's as a 'fading shadow of democracy' while Obi concludes that the multi-party system is 'prising the people out of politics.' These views represent the feeling of many African voters. See Ake, *Democracy and Development in Africa* and *Democratisation of Disempowerment in Africa*, CASS Occasional Monograph, Lagos: Malthouse, 1994; Mkadawire, 'Crisis Management and the Making of 'Choiceless Democracies' in Africa,' in Richard Joseph (ed.), *The State, Conflict and Democracy in Africa*, Boulder CO: Lynne Rienner, 1999. See also Adejumobi, 'Elections in Africa,' and Obi, *No Choice, But Democracy*.

tion. In many places in Africa, including Kenya, the ballot has failed to deliver meaningful democracy. It is because of this repeated failure that we counterpoise the ballot box with the street. We treat both as sites of electoral contest with varying degrees of legitimacy.

The legitimacy of the ballot box over the street is conditional upon the former satisfying its role. The ballot box ought to facilitate the free and fair exercise of choice. In the absence of impartiality in electioneering and fair choice at balloting, the ballot box becomes fair game. In other words, an abused ballot box mimics the character of the street in terms of the resulting uncertainty. Streets are rather uncertain places for deciding representation.[38] They are sites of protest: they kick in when the ballot fails.

The street is a place of uncertainty, useful and acceptable when conforming to state dictates and sanctions but unlawful when mobilised to challenge illegitimately deployed power. In a system characterised by impunity and widespread abuse of the law, decisions on the lawfulness of street action cannot be decided by the state singly. This decision is less about the law and more about who decides what is lawful. In such cases, it does not matter whether the means of protest are peaceful or disorderly; the aim of protest influences the process.[39] In other words, the contrast between the ballot box and street refers to a way of thinking about the legitimacy of institutionalised mechanisms of managing competitive politics. Here, the distinction between lawful and unlawful acts is blurred.

Additionally, one must specifically appreciate that the 'logic of [street] violence' embeds a complex dynamic[40] that does not easily follow a definite sequence of events or precise order of performance. Violent protest of the kind witnessed in Kenya is not simply a moral issue of determining when killers attacked innocent victims, it is also about how the political struggle moved from the balloting box to the streets, from simple disagreement to murderous violence. Streets are messy spaces of rebuttal. They are susceptible to abuse, chaos and disorder. This characterisation is no less the product of the innate habits of street crowds than it is the consequence of official criminalisation of protests. How electoral dispute moved from the balloting space to the street is therefore central to the crisis in Kenya.

---

38. I use the notion of the street in a generic sense to refer to 'unauthorized' spaces where post-election protests and violence took place.

39. One can count how many street protests have been permitted as lawful by the Kenyan state. The negligible number of lawful protests has remained even after Mwai Kibaki, a prime beneficiary of street-based mass action against the Moi/KANU regime, came to power.

40. Stathis N. Kalyvas as cited in Daniel Branch, *Defeating Mau Mau, Creating Kenya: Counterinsurgency, Civil War, and Decolonization*, Cambridge: Cambridge University Press, 2009, p. 10. See also Kalyvas, 'The Ontology of "Political Violence": Action and Identity in Civil Wars,' in *Perspectives on Politics*, vol. 1, no. 3, 2003, pp. 475–94.

When it is not abused, the ballot box is a better place for achieving governance. It is invested with constitutional authority and can be easily disciplined to operate within the framework of law and order. Three conditions are identified as necessary to satisfy the effectiveness and legitimacy of electoral administration. They include the independence and neutrality of the election management body; impartiality; transparency and security of tenure. These conditions are important in preventing electoral contests from spilling on to the street. In Kenya, these were not satisfied. In fact, it is argued that 'electoral malpractices may have been systematically planned.'[41]

The streets exist in marked contrast with the ballot box. They constitute unregulated public spaces often thought of in terms of lawlessness and disorder. The street is susceptible to abuse. It is the place to go when the idea is to challenge illegitimate law. In other words, it is in the nature of an electoral contest that a perceived unfairness can shift the base of action from the ballot box to the street.

Though streets are not the legalised forum for contesting election results or for instituting change against a flawed mandate, they are legitimate sites of politics of protest. Protests do not draw their legitimacy from conforming to the dictates of the state, they justify their means by reference to their just causes. In this function, they are often contrasted with the courts. The contrast is, however, irredeemably flawed in places where courts are themselves on trial for obstructing just causes. In Kenya, courts are notorious for their multiple failures as institutions of justice.[42] In several instances in Kenya's momentous history of reform, street protests became justified avenues for challenging Moi's misrule. But a number of analysts do not agree that there was just cause in using protests to challenge Kibaki's flawed mandate: for them, violence is simply a part of Raila Odinga's way of doing things.[43]

---

41. Andreassen, et. al., 'I Acted Under a Lot of Pressure', p. 29.

42. Makau Mutua, 'Justice under Siege: The Rule of Law and Judicial Subservience in Kenya,' in *Human Rights Quarterly*, vol. 23, no. 1, 2001, pp. 96–118.

43. The insinuation that violence is simply in Raila Odinga's DNA was largely found in pedestrian discussions online or bar-room conversations. It, however, found its way into write-ups by otherwise credible authors. Peter Kimani implies it in his argument that 'power "by any means necessary" is a mantra that perfectly fits Odinga.' See his 'A Past of Power More than Tribe in Kenya's Turmoil,' Open Democracy http://www.opendemocracy.net/article/a_question_of_power_before_tribes posted on 01-02-2008 (browsed on 19 October 2009).

Box I: Protest and the Example of the Orange Revolution

Street action is legitimate action where regular avenues of redress over electoral or related disputes are compromised or obstructed. In Kenya, these avenues were compromised and obstructed to facilitate Kibaki's second term. Thus, once the incumbent was sworn in, the legitimacy of the ballot box was irreparably undermined. Worse, the declaration of the winner was followed by a sneaky swearing-in ceremony and a ban on live media broadcast. Not only did this obstruct public discussion, it altered the nature of any possible discussions of what was happening. Consequently, street protests took over and became alternative bases of contest. It was the hope of some protesters, and especially those aligned with ODM, that this would become an alternative way of effecting change. Indeed, ODM seemed to style itself in the manner of the Orange Revolution in Ukraine, promising to mobilise one million people to enthrone Raila Odinga as a people's president. It utterly failed to realise this objective because the state deployed police power that blocked any attempts at protest. Furthermore, there was significant difference in style, context and personalities in ODM as compared with the real Orange Revolution.

In Ukraine, the Orange Revolution had similar aims of delegitimising the compromised ballot box and bringing to power the rightful winner of the election. But the only valid comparison between Ukraine and Kenya was the blatant way in which elections had been rigged by the incumbent and the spontaneous response of people. In Ukraine, the opposition party leader Viktor Yushshenko carried with him a sound record of reform both in his days as a banker and as prime minister. Though a lot more progressive than most Kenyan politicians, Raila Odinga had not attained a comparable profile, since he had no radical reform record in his KANU or NARC days, perhaps because the opportunity was circumscribed. Worse, his reformist inclination was undermined by the anti-reform ex-KANU politicians around him in ODM. Most of them, like those around Kibaki, were guilty of years of undermining the struggle for reform. Kenya's 'Orange Revolution' was therefore stillborn. It was foiled when it emerged that some ODM hardliners were implicated in pre-planned violence, violence that also compromised the demands of the genuine protestors and emptied the protests of their social content.

See Adrian Karatnycky, 'Ukraine's Orange Revolution,' in *Foreign Affairs*, vol. 84, no. 2, 2005.

Forms of Post-Election Violence

There are several studies on PEV in Kenya. The outstanding contribution, both in terms of breadth of coverage and attention to detail, is the report of the Commission of Inquiry into Post-Election Violence (CIPEV) chaired by Judge Philip N. Waki, and the Kenya National Committee on Human Rights (KNHCR) Reports. Other studies, less deep and wide in coverage but still very informative, include the report of Human Rights Watch (HRW) and the International Crisis Group (ICG). There are also other studies on specific aspects of the violence, whose veracity varies according to the predilections of their authors.[44] These studies constitute important sources of data that inform the discussion in this section. This literature identifies three forms of violence in post-election Kenya, spontaneous, planned/premeditated and state-directed violence.

Spontaneous Protest and Violence

Spontaneous riots and protests were the first to occur. These protests were extensive, giving credence to the view that post-election situation was primarily a social revolt against a state instituted *coup d'état*.[45] In general, protests took place immediately after the announcement of Kibaki as 'winner' of the 2007 presidential vote and were mainly against the blatant rigging of elections and swearing in of Kibaki for a second five-year term. Anger was heightened by the fact that irregularities that added up to manipulation of tallies were revealed, contested and played out in the national media days after the actual voting. Further, the swearing in of Kibaki took place in a most sneaky manner in the privacy of State House in Nairobi, suggesting that he had something to hide. Not only did the swearing-in happen at night, it took place in the absence of the usually choreographed media glamour and the invited dignitaries, including foreign ambassadors that often grace such occasions. One could see on television a select few in attendance, some of them previous ministers, a good number of whom had lost in the just ended elections, including Raphael Tuju and Musikari

---

44. CIPEV Report; International Crisis Group, *Kenya in Crisis*, Africa Report no.137, 21 February 2008; Human Rights Watch, *Ballots to Bullets Organized Political Violence and Kenya's Crisis of Governance*, HRW Report, vol. 20, no. 1, March 2008; KNCHR, *On The Brink of the Precipice: A Human Rights Account of Kenya's Post-2007 Election Violence*, 15 August 2008; Johan de Smedt, "'No Raila, No Peace!' Big Man Politics and Election Violence at the Kibera Grassroots,' in *African Affairs*, vol. 108, no. 433, 2009, pp. 581–98; Anderson and Lochery, 'Violence and Exodus in Kenya's Rift Valley'; Maupeu, 'Revisiting Post-Election Violence,' in Jérôme Lafargue (ed.), *The General Elections in Kenya, 2007*, Dar es Salaam: Mkuki na Nyota, 2009; Klopp and Kamungi, 'Violence and Elections.'

45. Firoze Manji, 'It is the Kenyan People Who Have Lost the Election,' posted at http://pambazuka.org/en/category/features/45203 2008-01-03, Issue 334 and Peter Anyang' Nyong'o, 'Ocampo Hour of Reckoning is Here, We Can't Beat any Retreat,' in *Daily Nation*, 5 November 2009.

Kombo. This swearing-in happened in a manner akin to that for then President Moi after the flawed elections of 1992 and 1997.

Violence was sparked off in large measure by the tense situation surrounding the electoral process and the thwarted expectations that Raila Odinga would win. It had been expected that if defeated, the incumbent would accede to the people's wishes. Indeed, the Kenyan military had been preparing for the official swearing-in ceremony, ideally to take place at the Uhuru Park grounds in Nairobi. These expectations had built over time, especially after the 2002 elections, when a smooth power transfer took place, and the 2005 referendum on the draft constitution, which saw the government humbly admitting defeat. During the electioneering, the sanctity of the ballot was defended and a chorus of voices against rigging was repeatedly heard. This was nothing unusual, as a similar chorus had been evident prior to the 2002 election. At the time, an explicit warning was given that if President Moi tampered with the results, the opposition would evict him from State House.

Some analysts have attributed the violent 2007 outcome to an exaggerated ODM campaign tactic that repeatedly warned against election rigging and called on supporters to be vigilant and to accept nothing less than an ODM win. While attributing this style to Dick Morris, the American campaign consultant, proponents argue that this strategy was simply meant to prepare the country for pre-planned violence, since it anticipated and accepted nothing other than an ODM win.[46] On the contrary, it is clear that expectations of a Raila Odinga win were not simply the consequence of ODM hyping its own popularity.

The popularity of ODM in most parts of the country compared to the Party of National Unity (PNU) is indisputable. This partly explains the widespread nature of the protests. It was evident not just in the lead that Raila Odinga built over Kibaki but also in the geographic spread of the ODM parliamentary and civic representation in Kenya. This popularity translated into an almost unassailable lead in the tallies reported by both the media and ECK in the two days before the violence. Though premature, this opened the way for celebrations in parts of the country where people anticipated the announcement of a Raila Odinga win. On the night of 29 December 2007, the lead was implausibly reduced as the state intervened and manipulated vote tallies to ensure Kibaki was declared winner.[47]

Suspicion of foul play was heightened when the media stopped reporting

---

46. See, for instance, Kimani, 'A Past of Power More than Tribe in Kenya's Turmoil'and Peter Mwangi Kagwanja, 'Breaking Kenya's Impasse: Chaos or Courts? *Africa Policy Brief*, no. 1, 2008, p. 6 found at http://www.africapi.org/siteimages/Africa_Policy_Brief_No.1_January_2008.pdf. Browsed on 26 September 2009.

47. Chaacha Mwita, *Citizen Power: A Different Kind of Politics, A Different Kind of Journalism*, Nairobi: Global Africa Corporation, 2009.

the provisional figures phoned in by their correspondents across the country. Instead, the ECK began to release results of the parliamentary vote, results normally counted and released after the presidential ones. ODM officials in the media centre in turn actively challenged the credibility of the results from specific constituencies and, in a number of cases, were backed up by international election observer teams, including most energetically the European Union team. In places where celebrations had commenced, such as Mombasa and Luo Nyanza, the festivities immediately turned into protests. In Mombasa, escalating 'tension, anxiety and fear' culminated in protests, blocking of roads and violence. This, according to the CIPEV Report, was due to 'the declaration of President Kibaki as the winner' and the 'suspicious manner' in which the ECK 'handled the situation.'[48]

The pattern of spontaneous violence was repeated in at least two other provinces. In Western province (with the exception of Lugari) and Nyanza (excluding Kisii), the initial violence 'was a direct consequence of political differences': it was spontaneous and directly 'flowed from disaffection with the final tally of the presidential results.'[49] Starting with bigger towns like Kakamega, Busia and parts of Bungoma to smaller ones like Kapsokwany (headquarters of Mt Elgon district), Mumias and Butere, the violence escalated from the time the results were announced and only abated a few days later. It spread and affected almost all the big towns, small markets, especially along the major road networks in the provinces, and in rural shopping centres.

In Luo Nyanza, the CIPEV Report identified three phases of this initial violence, all of which relate in some way to acts of protest against the presidential results, the excessive use of brutal and fatal police force and, finally, against the targeting of Luos by militia in Nakuru and Naivasha districts. The most striking phase is the first, which was due to the declaration of Kibaki as winner. It took place over three days starting the 29 December 2007.

It must be understood that in Luo Nyanza, perhaps unlike many other pro-ODM regions, the emotional investment in a Raila Odinga presidency had been palpable. This is understandable and is not an exception. Even in Central province, which is populated by Kibaki's Gikuyu ethnicity, there was equal emotion invested in a Kibaki win. For the Luo, however, this was the very first time that someone of Luo ethnicity had a credible shot at the presidency.[50] It is therefore not unusual that protests in Luo Nyanza began a day ahead of the announce-

---

48. CIPEV Report, pp. 225–6.
49. CIPEV Report, p. 174.
50. This even invited comparisons with the US elections in which the question was raised as to which country, the US or Kenya, would be the first to have a Luo president. See BBC, 'Could US elect a Luo before Kenya?' http://news.bbc.co.uk/2/hi/africa/7170089.stm (browsed 26 October 2009).

ment of the winner. At this time, the delay in releasing the results was generally construed as vote manipulation at the tallying centre. This possibility grew in plausibility as a result of the behaviour of the ECK and the altercation at the media centre in Nairobi between parties and with the ECK. The ECK chairman not only 'hinted' that some returning officers had delayed relaying the tally back to Nairobi, he actually stated clearly at a press conference that some of his returning officers had 'gone missing' and that he had asked the police to locate them. He insinuated they might be involved in 'cooking' the results and warned them against such action. This heightened tensions in the country, especially in Luo Nyanza, where violence was reported on 29 December 2007 in several towns in Rachuonyo, Migori, Siaya and Nyando districts. When the 'winner' was declared, the whole of Nyanza was engulfed in protests and violence that continued until 31 December.

The other provinces that experienced extended violence were Nairobi and Rift Valley, but it is not easy to distinguish the spontaneous protests from the premeditated violence, because of the widespread mix of forms of violence that occurred there. We cannot totally rule out genuine protest against flawed elections, though these must have been few and overshadowed. The CIPEV Report concludes that in the South Rift region, especially in Sotik/Borabu and Kipkelion, 'violence, initially spontaneous, increasingly showed signs of organisation, the longer it went on.' The report attributes the spontaneous aspect to 'disaffection with the election results or perceived illegitimacy of the process' by which the winner was determined.[51]

To some degree, the targets of initial spontaneous violence in Coast, Western and Nyanza indicate the motives of protestors. In Western province, roads were blocked and shops razed, while in Nyanza government property was set alight. The aim, it seems, was to give vent to popular anger against government by crippling its or related operations. In most urban places in these regions, protestors collected every item in sight, including boulders and items from shops, and used them to block the roads. At times, they proceeded to light up fires on the roads, thereby blocking them and damaging the tarmac. This contrasts with places in the Rift Valley, where trees were systematically cut down and used to block the roads. By seeking to cripple government operations, protesters aimed to put government under pressure, hoping that the hardliner politicians around the presidency, like Martha Karua, Michuki and Amos Kimunya, would relent and allow for transparent verification of results. In Western province, for example, most market towns along the Kakamega to Busia, Webuye to Kakamega, Webuye to Bungoma and Webuye to Busia roads were marked by destruction and looting, with all the roads rendered impassable.

---

51. CIPEV Report, pp. 161–2.

In Luo Nyanza, citizen anger was directed at government offices and property. This was due to 'a perception that the polls had been rigged by government agents', a perception not altogether unfounded given that the Administrative Police had been trained in election rigging in parts of the country, especially in Nyanza.[52] The provincial administration and related government functionaries were also targeted. Several government vehicles were set ablaze, as were specific businesses owned by those perceived to be PNU supporters.

Following this violence, roads were closed for awhile as police tried to restore order. But as the details of the extent of protest, damage and violence mounted, it became clear the country had been brought to a halt, except perhaps in North-Eastern, Eastern and Central provinces, where ODM had limited influence. Not only had the police been overwhelmed, most of them had been dispatched to quell violence in places where they were least needed, leaving the most serious trouble spots of criminal violence insufficiently policed. They therefore failed to provide security to the most vulnerable in Nairobi and the Rift Valley provinces, while Luo Nyanza seemed to have received reinforcements that turned out, as I argue below, to be murderous police squads targeting innocent people. This has become the most tragic police miscalculation in the PEV.

Cumulatively, spontaneous protest and violence served to drive home the point that votes only count when they are counted equally. There was also a geopolitical dimension to this that shocked many, including the ECK commissioners and those others who choreographed Kibaki's flawed second mandate. Some Kibaki lieutenants had reportedly adopted a very cynical attitude towards violence. They calculated on sacrificing a few members of 'the Kikuyu internal Diaspora in the Rift Valley' 'in order to advance [their] agenda' nationally.[53] They were shocked both at the spontaneity of the riots and protests and the extent of their occurrence, not just in the Rift Valley and Nyanza where they had correctly assumed violence would occur, but also in Coast and Western provinces, where they expected resigned acceptance of Kibaki's re-election. This geopolitical factor is perhaps the most important issue in considering the negotiation that led to a power-sharing arrangement. Though Kibaki and Raila Odinga may have bagged almost equal votes, their geographical spread indicated that Kibaki's votes came mostly from his Central province backyard and the Gikuyu-inhabited sections of Rift Valley, while Raila's were spread across most of Western, Rift Valley, Nyanza and Coast provinces. In terms of inter-ethnic

---

52. *The Star*, 3 August 2009; *Standard*, 10 and 11 April 2010; CIPEV Report, pp.407–12.
53. This statement is attributed to Prof. Joel D. Barkan and Maina Kiai. See Kevin J. Kelley, 'US team says "flawed" poll results now irreversible,' in *The East African*, 14 January 2008 or (http://www.theeastafrican.co.ke/news/-/2558/257586/-/t67e6pz/-/index.html browsed on 3 November 2009.

mobilisation, Raila held a firm and convincing command that left Kibaki's mandate limited in geographical scope.

The widespread protests and danger they posed for post-election governance forced the international community to support the post-election power-sharing arrangement. In Nigeria and Ethiopia, for instance, observers declared the results flawed but the 'winners' were sworn in and continue to occupy office in spite of the condemnations of the international community. But in Kenya, Kibaki was forced into a power-sharing arrangement that eroded some of his executive power.[54]

With time, protagonists in the post-election drama who were happy to have the police and protesters battling it out lost control of their foot soldiers. It is at this point that one begins to witness widespread looting, burning and evictions. These intermediate acts illustrate how protests morphed into criminal murders. Let us briefly highlight the character of these acts.

Premeditated or Planned Violence

Prelude to Premeditated Violence

The prelude to premeditated violence was characterised by intermediate acts that may have been violent but were not necessarily planned in advance. This violence should be distinguished from planned violence, which involved prior planning and better coordination. Though there is evidence of planning dotted all over the Rift Valley, these were acts of pure harassment, threats of violence, the targeting of specific peoples and communities and their temporary or permanent expulsion from their homes. These, combined with looting and the burning of shops, occupy that ambiguous in-between space between simple protest and intentional virulent violence.

As stated earlier, the line between spontaneous and premeditated violence was imprecise at best. Specific threats of violence and targeting of communities were reported in Nairobi's informal settlements and slum areas, in Western and Coast provinces, in Luo Nyanza and in parts of the Rift Valley, but most of these cases did not, initially, constitute a premeditated desire to evict or kill.

---

54. On the Ethiopian elections, see the review of books on the topic by Berhanu Abegaz, 'The 2005 Ethiopian Elections: Millstone or Milestone?' in *Africa Review of Books*, vol. 3, no. 1, 2007. On contrasts between Kenya and Ethiopia, see Lahra Smith, 'Explaining Violence after Recent Elections in Ethiopia and Kenya,' in *Democratization*, vol. 16, no. 5, 2009, pp. 867–97. For a review of the Nigerian case, see Jibrin Ibrahim, 'Nigeria's 2007 Elections: The Fitful Path to Democratic Citizenship,' Special Report no. 182, 2007, United States Institute of Peace. Available at http://www.usip.org/pubs/specialreports/sr182.html browsed 28 September 2009; Cyril I. Obi, 'International Election Observer Missions and the Promotion of Democracy: Some Lessons from Nigeria's 2007 Elections,' in *Politikon*, vol. 35, no. 1, 2008, pp. 69–86 and J. Shola Omotola, '"Garrison" Democracy in Nigeria: The 2007 General Elections and the Prospects of Democratic Consolidation,' in *Commonwealth and Comparative Politics*, vol. 47, no. 2, 2009, pp. 194–220.

They simply fed into a localised logic driven by petty jealousy and rivalries and a settling of old scores. This was a form of targeting the CIPEV Report categorised as 'unplanned' but which Arne Tostensen describes as acts arising from a tense and easy-to-manipulate situation.[55] It involved public outbursts whose intention might simply have been to mock or scare others but lacked the impetus to do much more. For instance, there were Kikuyu assertions that *wajaluo wajipange* (Luo should be prepared to move) or at the Coast where people *watoka bara* or *wabara* (from upcountry) were isolated.[56]

This mild hate speech did not immediately upset the peace or lead to violence. In Nairobi, this ambiguous phase was characterised by exceptional acts by neighbours to protect the property of others of different ethnicity. This remained true until pressure from adjoining areas precipitated the breakout of violence. Before matters got out of control, some Kikuyu landlords in Mathare North provided housing for evicted people from other estates in Nairobi. Interviews conducted for the Kenya Thabiti Taskforce testify that peace prevailed in Ngei Estate, for instance, where Luo youths initially protected 'Kikuyu properties' until 'reports' came through that two Luo had been killed. This gave rise to the suspicion that broke the initial peace in Kia Michael and Ngei areas.[57] Thus, peace prevailed in select areas in Nairobi until word of inter-ethnic killings and mild hate speech filtered into the local rumour mill. From these mild tensions, the way was paved for attacks on specific communities.

When this hate speech gave way to attacks in Western and Nyanza, those perceived as PNU supporters, whether Gikuyu or not, became victims. Of course, the Gikuyu were presumed to be pro-PNU and therefore suffered the greatest consequence, but also included were other people, especially aspirants who had run for election on the PNU ticket at civic and parliamentary levels or were seen as supporting the party. Some, like Prof. Ruth Oniang'o from Butere constituency, had their projects and properties destroyed in the ensuing mêlée, even though these projects were meant to support local communities. In Rift Valley and Nyanza, the Kisii were similarly harassed in Kisumu and Kericho towns, while in the second week of January 2008, word went out that the Luo should prepare to flee Kericho town if Raila Odinga agreed to negotiate with Kibaki.[58] In general, a good number of those targeted were forced to flee their homes and businesses and relocate to neighbouring countries. Some chiefs and aspirants in

---

55. See Arne Tostensen, 'Electoral Mismanagement and Post-Election Violence in Kenya: The Kriegler and Waki Commissions of Inquiry,' *Nordic Journal of Human Rights*, vol. 27, no. 4, 2009, pp. 445.

56. CIPEV Report, pp. 118, 221

57. Focus Group Interview for Kenya Thabiti Taskforce conducted by Mshai Mwangola and Bosire at NCCK Centre in Huruma on Wednesday, 20 April 2008.

58. This came from discussion I had with touts at a petrol station in Kericho town on the 8ᵗ January 2008.

Nyanza fled across the border into Tanzania while some Gikuyu in Western fled into Uganda. A good number moved into police stations or IDP camps.

Makeshift camps were hurriedly erected at local police stations to accommodate IDPs. In a number of instances, businesses and houses belonging to Gikuyu were looted and burned. Those caught in the fires were the tenants who rented houses belonging to these landlords. In other cases, these houses were simply looted, leaving behind empty shells. The looted property most certainly belonged to tenants, many of whom were locals. Occasionally, looting went beyond the Gikuyu to include rich businesses owned by locals or by people of Asian ancestry, including hardware shops in rural markets. In Kisumu, extensive looting of stores owned by businessmen of Asian ancestry was broadcast on television. Where possible, such owners hired locals to guard and protect their property as they sought refuge elsewhere.

It is in the example of the looting, harassment and theft that the post-election crisis shows a shift from simple protest to apparently planned criminal acts. Theft and looting were, however, intimately tied to local political dynamics: in some cases, simple jealousy and petty rivalries among neighbours were involved, and in others, unemployed youths took advantage of the lawlessness and disorder to loot property. This resulted in muggings, robbery, vandalism and arson in peri-urban areas of Kisumu, for instance. According to a speaker at the inaugural Gender Forum Session for Western Kenya organised by the Heinrich Böll Foundation, the violence and looting were also a consequence of idleness among the youth in Kondele, who harboured great bitterness at the lack of opportunities for advancement.[59]

In other words, the range of reasons for looting and violence grew as the days wore on and as the violence escalated from a mostly local to a national phenomenon. Though this had everything to do with the opportunity provided by the post-election crisis, not all this violence was planned as murderous acts of ethnic cleansing. In Western, Luo Nyanza and Coast province, as well as in selected instances in Nairobi, this violence constituted the interface between spontaneous protest and planned violence.[60] This would also explain why in these places, excluding Nairobi, the highest numbers of deaths and injuries were caused by the police, while citizen-to-citizen deaths were considerably fewer.

---

59. These views on Kisumu are attributed to contributors to a workshop organised by the Heinrich Böll Foundation in Kisumu on Wednesday, 30 April 2008. Report of workshop prepared by Easter Achieng' of Kenya Female Advisory Organisation (KEFEADO) is in the custody of this author. Thanks to Wanjiku Wagoki for sharing the report of the meeting.

60. The CIPEV Report felt constrained to admit that in the Rift Valley 'an aspect of the violence was spontaneous, and that the disaffection with the election results or the perceived illegitimacy of the process could have been as [sic] the cause of the violence.' See CIPEV Report, p. 161.

Premeditated Violence

Planned violence involved organised groups, often engaged in brutal acts, including murder. They acted in a manner that reveals levels of coordination that cannot be coincidental or achieved spontaneously. This form of violence was less geopolitically widespread in post-election Kenya. Instead, it targeted clearly identified victims either on the basis of presumed party affiliation and/or ethnicity. Lasting a little longer than the spontaneous protests, it involved more fatalities. It, moreover, combined outright criminality with those other acts that straddle criminality and protest. This violence had more horrific implications for victims and for the country's stability and occurred mostly in the Rift Valley and in Nairobi, where groups of people were mobilised.

In the Rift Valley, planning should be thought of in two ways. There was pre-election planning of violence and post-election planning for revenge. In North and South Rift, pre-election planning dominated. There is evidence of planning for violence before the election or soon after the initial protests subsided. While it has been suggested that such violence was bound to happen, irrespective of which presidential candidate won, its scale was, however, underestimated by many and, partly because of this, the horror that came with it remains unspeakable. This violence grew out of earlier acts and continued, even though in sporadic spurts, after the initial protests. The case that PEV was primarily a social protest is consequently undermined in the eyes of critics, who correctly point out that protests should ideally aim to protect the poor and vulnerable rather than kill, maim and displace them in the name of fighting for democracy.

In the Rift Valley and sections of Nairobi, the logic of protecting the poor did not apply. Instead, what we see is the complex dynamic of violence and war highlighted earlier in the paper. The perpetrators of violence rather indiscriminately targeted people of Gikuyu ethnicity, few of whom were members of the political class and the majority of whom were poor farmers, women and children. Not only was the violence aimed at expelling them from their homes, it included rape and murder of a most foul nature.

In Nakuru and Naivasha districts of Central Rift, however, much of the violence was of the post-election revenge type. It was couched as revenge against those from communities considered to have been involved in the initial violence. This violence, like the organised murders before them, had all the hallmarks of political mobilisation to settle old scores and proceeded on the assumption that victims were guilty due to their ethnic affiliation. Thus, like the original violence, revenge attacks failed in their own logic, since those upon whom revenge was visited were not the original perpetrators and neither were they the political elite responsible for election rigging.

To mitigate the sense of guilt, perpetrators had imagined and de-humanised likely victims through hate speech and other appellations in advance of the violence. This reduced the victims' humanity and objectified them.[61] As a further strategy, an easy slippage was allowed into the discourse that interchanged 'individual persons' with 'ethnic' references. The slippage came to colour everyday talk and, as a consequence, it became clear that while individuals were human and perhaps an unjustified target of hatred and murder, their community was not. Instead, the community became a worthy target of hate and murder. At this level, it was no longer simply individual neighbours with specific names and rights to life: rather, victims simply became 'Kikuyus'. As 'Kikuyus', they could be depicted as *madoa doa* or *makwekwe* (weeds) or any other appellation that made the act of uprooting them from the Rift Valley by whatever means fathomable.[62]

The reduction of the Gikuyu, in particular, to a state of non-beings/non-belonging others happened prior to voting day and continued after. A similar logic applied in other places like Coast, Western and Nyanza, but not with the murderous virulence evident in the Rift Valley. In the Rift Valley, attacks on the Gikuyu (and to a lesser extent the Kisii) were justified by the simple logic that they voted, as every other Gikuyu was pejoratively considered to have done, for Kibaki. Since Kibaki and PNU politicians were perceived as responsible for the rigged elections, 'their' supporters did not deserve to live in 'our' midst.[63] In other words, being 'other' was enough justification for death.

Jackson Kibor's admission of this in an interview with BBC reporter Pascale Harter in Eldoret on 25 February 2008 perhaps captures the logic in its gruesome detail.[64] Elsewhere in the South Rift and Kisii regions, the violence reflected 'an attempt to exact retribution' against those locals felt were responsible for the 'loss by voting in a manner inconsistent with their [locals'] own voting patterns.' The CIPEV Report describes the resulting violence as 'a form of vicarious vengeance' against those the local Kipsigis community felt presided over a system that robbed them of an electoral victory.[65] Similar arguments were

---

61. The strategy of 'reducing the reality of humanness' is common in the security industry. Indeed, this thinking dominates the current securitisation of foreign policy, where notions of 'collateral damage' and 'precision bombing' have come to represent a sanitisation of war and death. See Yvonne A. Owuor 'Contemporary Projections: Africa in the Literature of Atrocity (Aftrocity),' in Okey Ndibe and Chenjerai Hove (eds), *Writers, Writing on Conflicts and Wars in Africa*, London and Uppsala: Adonis and Abbey Publishers and Nordic Africa Institute, 2009, p. 21.

62. CIPEV Report, p. 65.

63. CIPEV Report, p. 83.

64. Listen to the interview http://www.youtube.com/watch?v=eG4rDSXr3us. In the interview, Kibor argues that people had to fight the Gikuyu because Kibaki is Gikuyu. Claiming that the Gikuyu are only one 'tribe' out of 41 in Kenya, he accused the Gikuyu of supporting Kibaki and wondered how one 'tribe' could defeat the others.

65. CIPEV Report, p. 161.

articulated in the interviews for the Kenya Thabiti Taskforce in Nairobi. When asked why the whole nation turned against the Gikuyu, respondents argued that 'we cannot reach State House. The Kibaki who is here is the one that I see. That might be my neighbour, but as for me, that is the Kibaki I see.'

Others went as far as to justify their refusal to pay rent to Gikuyu landlords, citing the fact that landlords overcharged rent and Kibaki did nothing to control it: *'Kibaki aliiba kura, na sisi basi tunakataa hatulipi rent. Nenda kwa Kibaki akusaidie. Si ni president wako.'* (Kibaki stole the votes, we refuse to pay rent. Go to Kibaki for assistance. Isn't he your president?).[66]

The Case of Violence in the Rift Valley

There were two broad categories of violence in the Rift Valley: premeditated/planned and revenge violence. The first peaked after the declaration of Kibaki as winner and was followed a month later by revenge attacks on those communities perceived to have evicted the Gikuyu in the initial protest. Much of the violence tended to be one way, that is, a dominant community in an area attacked the other without any effective resistance. But there was an intermediate form of antagonism and violence in areas where contending communities fought each other because they were almost evenly matched. This form started before the elections and continued afterwards.

Pre-election planned violence in the Rift Valley predominated in Kalenjin-dominated areas, especially in North Rift. Here, the most callous violence occurred in Uasin Gishu and Trans Nzoia districts. It climaxed with the incident at the church at Kiambaa on 1 January 2008, during which 17 people were killed, 11 of them dying on their way to hospital.[67] Much of this violence tended to be one way, committed largely by groups of Kalenjin against their Gikuyu neighbours. In a few places in Central Rift, especially Koibatek district, the violence was therefore 'distinguishable.' This was the only district in Central Rift where 'violence was committed mostly by members of the Kalenjin community against members of the Gikuyu and Kisii communities, without much retaliation.'[68]

These attacks were primarily citizen-on-citizen and, at times, involved neighbours, some whom knew each other well. Many unsuspecting victims were left wondering how things had got this bad. Testimonies of victims illustrate the horror and surprise at the callousness of the perpetrators, especially in instances where children, old people and women were hacked to death, raped or extremely humiliated and dehumanised. Joseph Mwangi Macharia's story captures it all.

---

66. Focus Group Interview for Kenya Thabiti Taskforce conducted by Mshai Mwangola and Bosire at NCCK Centre in Huruma on Wednesday 20 April 2008.
67. CIPEV Report, pp. 48–9.
68. CIPEV Report, p. 93.

His family was attacked by a group of about 40 people who overran his household in Kesses location and killed seven members of his family. Among the attackers were his neighbours, whom he recognised.[69]

In this incident, as in others, the attackers used blunt objects to beat, arrows and spears to stab, machetes and *pangas* to slit and *rungus* to beat their victims. There is nothing obviously premeditated about this except in the number of perpetrators. A good number of them were transported by lorries to the scene of murder. The use of petrol to torch houses was a useful indicator of planning or premeditation, as it meant that perpetrators bought this flammable liquid in advance to burn houses. This is how the Kiambaa church was burned down. The fact that it was groups of organised people conducting the attacks and arson, that they had weapons acquired in advance of the violence and that some were ferried long distances in lorries indeed suggests coordination and planning.

In Central Rift, except Koibatek, the violence was evenly matched with communities fighting it out. Central Rift has an extensive ethnic mix and was a site of serious gerrymandering during the Moi era. This history of electoral malpractice is very relevant to what happened in 2007–08. Central Rift is host to Gikuyu, Kalenjin, Kisii, Maasai, Luyia communities and the other minority communities like the Ogiek. The latter have a historical claim to the Mau forest reserve in the Central Rift. This has been a source of tension between them and the Maasai on one hand and with the Kipsigis on the other hand. The axes of tension in the area are therefore many, contrary to the current focus on only the Kalenjin versus Gikuyu. Tensions also include those between the Maasai and the Kipsigis sub-ethnic group of the Kalenjin, which played out in 2008 in the Kilgoris by-election in Trans Mara district. These fault lines are the least explored, as many analysts focus on the Gikuyu/Kalenjin tensions, perhaps because they compel more attention.[70]

Molo region has always been the hot spot for violence in this area, and has been called the 'smouldering cauldron of Kenyan politics.'[71] Kuresoi constituency has of late been the hottest spot in the region. It was hived off from Molo by the Moi government in order to create a Kalenjin-dominated constituency. In Molo, the Gikuyu were the majority. Not only did they manage to elect their preferred MPs throughout the multi-party era, to Moi's consternation, but they also defended themselves periodically against Kalenjin attacks. By hiving off

69. CIPEV Report, p. 47.

70. This concern came up repeatedly in an interview I conducted with Kiplangat Cheruiyot of the Ogiek Peoples Development Programme in Nakuru on 29 August 2008. We revisit this faultline in a subsequent publication.

71. Hervé Maupeu, 'Revisiting Post-Election Violence,' in Joreme Lafargue, ed. *The General Elections in Kenya, 2007*, Dar es Salaam: Mkuki na Nyota, 2009, p. 204. The chapter also generally discusses violence in the Molo district.

Kuresoi, the Moi government created space for the Kalenjin electorate to vote for their Kalenjin parliamentarian and also galvanised them into intensified attacks on the minority Gikuyu.

The tensions and flare-up of conflict between Kalenjin and Gikuyu in the Central Rift is unique because it recurs throughout the electoral cycle. In the last cycle, there were reports of low-key attacks and counter-attacks throughout, pitting Kalenjin against Gikuyu and Gusii. These peaked during the 2005 constitutional referendum, but skirmishes continued through 2006 and 2007. Just before the election in December 2007, several places in Kuresoi were already hosting IDPs following hostile confrontations in the area. At least 20 people had been killed and over 200 houses burned down. The Catholic Justice and Peace Commission called for mobile voting stations in the area. Even Raila Odinga, in an opinion piece, cited Kuresoi and Mt Elgon as demonstrating the alarming 'spate of violence, killings and ethnic cleansing that was sweeping the nation' as elections neared. He linked this to government laxity and failure to rein-in politically-instigated violence.[72]

Indeed, the government had been reluctant or unwilling to intervene not just in Kuresoi but also in Mt Elgon, where the Saboat Land Defence Force terrorised locals. In Kuresoi, Kalenjin attacks targeting Gikuyu communities increased, thereby preparing the way for post-election violence. The attacks following the declaration of Kibaki as winner were coordinated and aimed at delivering the final blows in the endless cycle of violence: they involved deaths and the burning of houses, especially of the Gikuyu and Gusii in the area.[73] The CIPEV Report confirms that there was 'credible' information these attacks were incited and sponsored by leading Kalenjin politicians in the area. The report specifically names Zakayo Cheruiyot, who had toured the area 'promising to end the violence if the Kikuyu voted for him.'[74]

Violent revenge predominated in the Gikuyu-dominated areas of the province, especially Nakuru and Naivasha districts. This violence was primarily perpetrated by Gikuyu youths against all those members of communities perceived to have victimised Gikuyu in the initial violent protests. There was little or no resistance from the victims of these attacks since they were overwhelmed by the sheer number of attackers.

This violence was planned after the election and followed on the initial protests discussed above. The evidence for this is cited not only in the CIPEV and

---

72. See *Daily Nation*, 5 December 2007, p. 9 and Raila Odinga, 'Rising Insecurity Worrying,' in *Daily Nation*, 4 December 2007.

73. CIPEV Report , pp. 84–5: KNCHR, *On the Brink of the Precipice; The Standard*, 6 December 2007, p. 14.

74. CIPEV report, p. 87.

KNCHR reports but also in newspaper reporting.[75] Planning took the form of strategising to mobilise militia groups like Mungiki and contributing money to buy weapons or to pay the militia. Among those raising funds were Gikuyu businessmen, professionals and politicians in Nakuru and Nairobi. Meetings were held in Nairobi, Juja, Naivasha and Meru.

The meetings, kept secret and only open to Gikuyu, whipped up a sense of being under siege among the Gikuyu. The pretext given was that these meetings were to raise money for IDPs, but this rang hollow since humanitarian support for the displaced was the subject of ongoing public and nationwide campaigns mounted by the media and other civil society groups, with the collection and disbursement of contributions effectively managed by the Kenya Red Cross.[76] The secrecy of these meetings was to allow only an inward-looking cast to be brought to this sense of siege. Indeed, the notion of 'forty-one tribes against one' (see Box II) widely cited to demonstrate the 'innocence' of the Gikuyu elite owes much to this siege mentality and serves to justify the acts of revenge as defensive. No wonder that from this point it was not long before the group involved assumed the role of 'protecting the community from attacks in the future.'[77] Under this guise, funds were raised to 'buy arms for self-defence.' just in case Kofi Annan's mediation efforts then under way failed. But in the event, these funds ended up supporting the revenge violence reported in Naivasha and Nakuru.

Like those who planned the North Rift violence, the architects of revenge spoke the language of community. This time, the victims were simply Luo, Luyia or Kalenjin without independent human existence outside their community. But revenge is a misnomer in this case, since those upon whom revenge was visited were not involved in the original violence or protests. The perpetrators of revenge are said to have been incited into action by stories relayed from Gikuyu areas by displaced persons bearing heart-rending narratives of suffering on the other side. However, for the so-called revenge acts to make sense, the perpetrators conflated 'individual' and 'ethnic community.' Revenge was directed at people not for their individual actions but as a result of 'their collective guilt' as members of communities guilty of attacks on the Gikuyu. Of course, it did not matter that such slippage in usage was only rationalisation. Those hacked down died as individuals and the community remained.

---

75. See for instance *Daily Nation*, 27 February 2008, pp. 14–15.

76. Muthoni Wanyeki, ARRF study.

77. See Michael Chege, 'Kenya: Back From the Brink? p. 133; See Kimani, 'A Past of Power More than Tribe in Kenya's Turmoil' and Kagwanja, 'Breaking Kenya's Impasse' on the notion of 'forty-one tribes against one' and *Daily Nation*, 27 February 2008, p. 14 on 'protecting the community' quote.

Box II: 'Forty-One Tribes Against One'

The notion of 'forty-one tribes against one' developed in the context of the 2007 general elections. It is shorthand to argue that all ethnic communities in Kenya ganged up on the Gikuyu during the elections. The potency of this claim, however, only comes through in the context of the PEV that engulfed the country after Mwai Kibaki was questionably declared winner of the presidential race. In this context, the statement assumes the character of a victims' claim to being unfairly harassed, hounded, evicted and murdered for simply exercising a democratic right. It is both a declaration of the innocence of the Gikuyu and an assertion of the guilt of all others.

But the statement is inaccurate and does not help to create peace in an ethnically fractured country. It ignores disputes over the number of ethnic groups constituting Kenya. Some, especially minority communities, still contest their elision in the ethnic count. Second, it wrongly assumes that only Gikuyu were targeted in the post-election violence. Not even the Gusii of Nyanza and the many others of different ethnicities variously harassed or discriminated against in different parts of the country, including non-Gikuyu in Central province, are included. More importantly, the fault lines of ethnic divisions, if indeed the divisions were only ethnic, were more complicated than is reflected in this calculation. The Kamba and communities in North-Eastern province neither allied with nor were they necessarily against the Gikuyu. Finally, in using the term 'tribes,' the statement is ignores its known pejorative connotations and the critiques in the literature on naming and representation.

This statement is a summation of those electioneering aspects the Gikuyu elite prioritised to galvanise support for themselves in the interest of preserving their hold on state power while falsely claiming their objective to be Gikuyu power. The assertion has two aims: to selectively emphasise aspects that showed the Gikuyu alone were victimised for exercising their democratic right to vote and to create fear and a sense of siege within the community. The net aim is to mobilise internal unity, unity that had been threatened by the emergence of lumpen militia groups like Mungiki that frustrated the Gikuyu elite's class interests. It is a polarising call to the Gikuyu to protect their community from other communities.

To be effective, the call relies on selective amnesia. What is remembered is that most other communities did not support Kibaki; that as a result, especially communities in the Rift Valley went on to institute hateful ethnic speech that reduced the mass of Gikuyu settlers into *madoa doa* (spots) or *makwekwe* (weeds) to be uprooted from their midst. When the political class around Kibaki abused the electoral process and disrupted the tallying of votes, groups of people, both in anger at the abuse but also as a result of prior planning, proceeded to commit violent acts and criminal murders against innocent Gikuyu voters leading to displacements and deaths. However, in seeking to galvanise the Gikuyu to protect their community, proponents of this statement in essence justified the murderous 'revenge' attacks that took place in late January 2008 in Naivasha and Nakuru district, in which similarly innocent people were killed.

The nature and distribution of deaths in post-election Kenya is a useful index for measuring the targets of violence. When analysed, they expose the patent exaggeration in the 'forty-one tribes against one' statement, a statement that seeks to exonerate and give the moral high ground to the Gikuyu political class, whose sense of entitlement to the presidency is partly the reason for the violence in the first place. A total of 1,133 people died. The highest number of deaths (278) were among the Luo, followed by 268 Gikuyu, 168 Luyia and 158 Kalenjin. The police bear the greatest responsibility for deaths, with 405 dying from gunshots. They mainly targeted Luo Nyanza, where 79.5% of deaths were from gunshots, followed by Western province (72.5%), Rift Valley (26%) and Nairobi (18.4%). Most of these were shot either in the back or the side. If indeed the post-election situation in Kenya was so clearly a case of 'forty-one tribes against one,' why do the statistics of the dead refuse to reflect this claim?

The Police and State-Directed Violence

State-sanctioned violence was carried out by state agents, mainly the Kenya Police, the Administrative Police and the General Service Unit. In some places, violence was coordinated through the provincial administration. At some point, the National Security Intelligence Service (NSIS) and the Kenyan Army were called in to play specified roles that entailed biasing the electoral field on behalf of Kibaki and PNU. While the CIPEV Report acquits the NSIS and army on grounds of their comparative preparedness, diligence and discipline, it reserves its harshest verdict for the others, concluding that 'police agencies quite simply … failed badly.'[78]

The police failed for several reasons, some related to their inextricable intimacy with the political class in government. The most important of these is

---

78. CIPEV Report, p. 374.

that they were part of the PNU's strategy to manipulate the elections.[79] About 1,607 Administrative Police were deployed on 24 December 2007 to Nyanza province. Having been influenced by certain people, including an ECK commissioner, their task was to manipulate the election results in favour of Kibaki. Indeed, it is precisely because of government control of the police that the latter exhibited such confidence in manipulating the electoral field and interfering with vote tallies. Both in the manner of their deployment and in the functions they were assigned, the Administrative Police and Kenya Police were meant to facilitate the defeat of the democratic process by tilting the electoral playing field and, if necessary, forcing a result that favoured Kibaki.

Along with the ECK, the police were responsible for the chaos in the tallying centre in Nairobi. Their presence at the KICC in exceedingly large number betrayed a motive other than simple provision of security. When incoming results were contested and evidence of inflated tallies provided, the police whisked the ECK chairman away, temporarily 'detaining' him in a room alone, whence he announced Kibaki as winner.

The announcement was recorded by the Kenya Broadcasting Corporation and relayed to a puzzled country. The ECK chairman was then whisked to State House, where he found Kibaki waiting for the certificate that confirmed him as winner. He was ready to be sworn in. On hand to facilitate this abrogation of the democratic process was Chief Justice Evan Gicheru. In the post-election disturbances, the police were again on hand to bludgeon people into silence and facilitate continuity of the Kibaki regime. With hindsight, it seems all preparations within the force prior to the elections were conducted with anti-democratic intent, disregarding the core task of protecting the most vulnerable in society. Signs of impending misplaced priorities can be gleaned in the period prior to voting.

Antecedents of Police Violence

In a modern state, the police are by definition a means of violence that can be used legitimately by the state. It does not follow, however, that such use is legitimate when deployed in favour of particular interests. In the Kenyan post-election situation, the police served partisan interests. Their role reflected their historical position as functionaries of the authoritarian Kenyan state. The force has functioned to secure the interests of the political class in government by silencing civic dissent, often with brute and murderous force. In the years following the Moi regime's defeat, a 'commitment' to police reform lulled many into believing the police were changing and would not be enticed into biasing

---

79. See CIPEV Report, pp.407–12; *Standard on Saturday*, 10 April 2010, pp. 12–13 and *Sunday Standard*, 11 April 2010, pp. 10–12.

the electoral field in 2007. Even some of the international community, including foreign aid agencies, moved to fund security-related reform programmes. The best known of these was the Governance, Justice, Law and Order Sector (GJ-LOS) programme. While the initial idea behind this was sound, GJLOS funds were ironically used to equip the Administrative Police, which perpetrated the worst post-election atrocities.

Reforms in the security sector were cosmetic at best. They included new appointments, periodic reshuffling and transferring of officers, modernising equipment and better equipping the force. The appointment of a military man, Major General Mohammed Hussein Ali, as commissioner of police, seemed to cap the changes. This was the first time in recent memory the head of police came from outside the force. The appointment attracted rave reviews, created hope of a new era in the police force and of a possible new relationship between police and citizens, which, according to some in civil society, was the area of greatest need.

Indeed, the police force under Moi, as under Kenyatta and the previous colonial government, had been the most visible cruel manifestation of the state. The force had wide discretionary powers to enforce the law and maintain security, which it used, in the colonial context, to control and brutalise people. With independence, not much changed: the authoritarian state that Kenyatta built and Moi inherited relied on force or threat of force to enforce compliance.[80] Over time, the force grew into an 'instrument for the political repression of the citizenry.'[81] It served the interests of the upper classes and provided little security for the general citizenry. It was a particularly useful instrument in repressing those demanding basic civil liberties and, in collaboration with the judiciary, helped entrench Moi's authoritarian rule.

With Major General Ali, the force was militarised. It distinguished itself by acts of extrajudicial, arbitrary and summary execution. The period preceding the December 2007 election was marked by worrying revelations of extrajudicial killings. These were obviously sanctioned by the state and targeted young men, especially those in the alleged Mungiki association. Mungiki is a banned vigilante group. For the police, the existence and activities of this association did not have to be proven in a court of law. They took it upon themselves to hunt,

---

80. See M. Tamarkin, 'The Roots of Political Stability in Kenya,' in *African Affairs*, vol. 77, no. 308, 1978 and also Boubacar N'Diaye, 'How Not to Institutionalize Civilian Control: Kenya's Coup Prevention Strategies, 1964–1997,' in *Armed Forces and Society*, vol. 24, no. 4, 2002.

81. J.M. Migai Akech, 'Public Law Values and the Politics of Criminal (In)justice: Creating a Democratic Framework for Policing in Kenya,' in *Oxford University Commonwealth Law Journal*, vol. 5, no. 2, 2005, p. 226. See also Edwin Gimode, 'The Role of the Police in Kenya's Democratisation Process,' in Godwin R. Murunga and Shadrack Nasong'o (eds), *Kenya: Struggle for Democracy*, London and Dakar: Zed Books in Association with CODESRIA, 2007.

kill and dump bodies in remote places in complete disregard of basic human rights. Many people disappeared in mysterious circumstances, while whistle-blowers who witnessed such executions were executed in cold blood.

The KNCHR investigated these killings and established police participation or complicity in them. They found decomposing bodies, bringing them to the attention of the police, who took no action. Eyewitness reports confirmed that the police killed people and dumped the bodies, and pictures of decomposing bodies are produced in the KNCHR reports. Such operations continued into and after the PEV, and marked the impunity associated with discretionary police powers. The government and police ignored, denied or dismissed the KNCHR reports until UN Special Rapportuer Prof. John Alston investigated and accorded the local reports international exposure and legitimacy.[82]

The actions of the police are not surprising as they fit the pattern of their work culture. What was new was the stamp of authority provided to their actions by Major General Ali. Ali was a smart and articulate commissioner, but also very easily captivated by his own meagre successes. Upon appointment, the force reduced crime by nearly 7 per cent in the first year. He revitalised and re-equipped the force and rescued it from collapse. In television interviews, he pronounced loftily on Kenya's security and intelligence matters, dismissing others as illiterate on the subject.

Ali was openly critical of civil society activists, dismissing them as lacking in knowledge of matters relating to law and order, and derisory about the whole activist enterprise. Activism, he believed, could not ensure peace, law and order for the country. His attitude towards civil society organisations was intolerant and contemptuous and he almost succeeded in turning everything into a referendum on whether these organisations had a right to speak on matters of security. In the process, he denied reports of police terror and murder and, one can safely assume, instructed police spokesman to similarly dismiss the veracity of the KNCHR findings.

Ali came across as a forceful policeman, indeed, as an embodiment of the masculine inclination to force and violence. Always straight-talking when threatening to invoke force, Ali also seemed aware of his unique status: that of the rare intelligent Kenyan police officer capable of intellectually defending himself and the force before any audience, including the media, whose reporters seemed dazzled by his performance. He radiated the confidence of an officer capable of controlling the law and order sector in such a way that the total good of all law-abiding and peace-loving Kenyans would be guaranteed.

---

82. See Press Statement by Prof. Philip Alston, UN Special Rapporteur on extrajudicial, arbitrary or summary executions Mission to Kenya 16–25 February 2009 at http://www.khrc. or.ke/ on 29 May 2009. Also see UN General Assembly Document A/HRC/11/NI/7 of 22 May 2009.

Back to PEV

But on the single question of security during elections, Ali got it all wrong. After repeatedly assuring Kenyans that security was guaranteed for law-abiding citizens during elections, the police force turned against Kenyans, earning the distinction of being the single sector most responsible for PEV deaths. They were accused of 'misplaced arrogance,' which led them to assume that they would 'always be able to control of what came up.' In relation to elections, this police attitude was 'simply too far off the mark.'[83] Not only were they the least prepared of the security agencies, they were badly coordinated and ended up inflicting the worst atrocities on innocent Kenyans.

Police (in)action during PEV stems from three interrelated conditions. First, they were deployed as a cog in the PNU election-rigging strategy, with the Administrative Police being recruited as PNU agents. Second, there was internal dissent and division in the force that compromised the chain of command and the force's effectiveness. Finally, even where regular officers were willing and ready to perform their tasks, they were either overwhelmed or too under-equipped to deliver.

This last point must be stressed. In the haste to blame, we often forget the diligent officers who successfully calmed crowds, intervened and saved lives, not to mention the many others who lost their lives while securing property or attempting to quell violence, such as Officer Ewafula Wakhungu in Uasin Gishu. The existence of such officers speaks to the resilience of responsible individuals in a force whose public image and credibility has been battered by the impunity of its leadership and corrupt rank-and-file officers.

Be that as it may, intelligence reports and public perception converge on the idea that the police force and provincial administration had been recruited into a PNU strategy to rig elections. If the violence in the North Rift was planned pre-election by ODM, police brutality in other parts was the PNU version of premeditated violence. Not only has it been confirmed that Administrative Police and NSIS were recruited for specific roles for PNU, it is also clear that deployment of the police force across the country was done to favour the incumbent: it was meant to silence dissent by brutalising voters in perceived ODM zones. Days before voting, several Administrative Police deployed to Nyanza to rig were killed by vigilant citizens, while a few escaped to tell their story.[84] They included William Nyamu, force number 2003052252, and George Mwangi Githuathi, force number 81010355, who died en route to serve as PNU agents. This forced the government to abandon their elaborate rigging plans using police. Only the NSIS acquitted itself competently in mapping possible scenarios

---

83. CIPEV Report, pp. 371–2.
84. See *The Standard on Saturday*, 10 April 2010, p. 12.

of violence and providing detailed information on lawlessness that could ensue. What is disturbing is the 'almost fatalistic realisation that no or insufficient preventive action would be taken to ameliorate the mayhem.'[85]

The police were unable to ameliorate the crisis because they did not use prevention to ensure citizen security. The CIPEV Report understood prevention to be a 'critical and fundamental element of policing' and placed the blame on the commissioner and top commanders for the 'failure to perform' preventive action.[86] Long after the violence, the lesson had still not been learned. Instead, the commissioner maintained that 'violence was unprecedented' and 'could not have been foreseen.'[87] This is despite of the fact that NSIS provided the requisite intelligence to facilitate preventive action to secure lives and property. Not only did the force fail to plan and prepare for the election, it also failed to take account of the intelligence received and information available on the ground and 'did not encompass preventive activities designed to reduce and/or ameliorate the impact of violence.'[88] By refusing to prepare in advance of the election, the police ended up using brutally misplaced force in an attempt to silence.

For historical reasons relating to the nature of the colonial and post-colonial state, the police prefer to react through force rather than prevent the occurrence of crime. The nature of the PEV deaths confirms this tendency. Of the 1,133 people who died, 405 died of gunshot wounds. An additional 557 of the 3,561 who sought medical treatment were treated for gunshot wounds.[89] The areas most affected by gunshot wounds are co-extensive with those perceived as pro-ODM. This 'coincidence' is too neat to require further confirmation that the police had murderous intent. In Nyanza alone, 89 of the 111 people reported dead were killed by gunshots. Of the 214 people admitted to hospitals in the province, 48 had gunshot wounds. Worse, a pathologist confirmed that of the 50 people shot in the region, 30 were shot from behind and nine from the side. Assuming these people were in flight, one wonders why the police used 'live bullets (or tear gas) on retreating crowds.'[90]

Some of the deceased were innocent women and children. Of the deceased in Nyanza, 3 were under 14 years and one old woman was shot while in her home. A similar situation obtained in Western province where, of the 98 deceased, 74 died of gunshot wounds. The CIPEV Report records 26 gunshot deaths of the total 31 in Kakamega, 11 of 12 in Mumias, 8 of 9 in Busia, 15 of 18 in Vihiga, and all 7 in Bungoma died of gunshot wounds. The same picture

---

85. CIPEV Report, p. 365.
86. CIPEV Report, pp. 377–8.
87. CIPEV Report, p. 371.
88. CIPEV Report, p. 371.
89. CIPEV Report, p. 386.
90. CIPEV Report, p. 389.

obtains for those who sought treatment. Less gruesome but similar statistics hold for the Rift Valley, where 170 of a total 779 died of gunshots. It is, however, clear that the scale of police killings declines as one ventures into the Rift Valley, where some regions were more affected than others. Statistics for Coast province indicate that of the 5 people who died, 4 were killed by gunshots and of the 22 admitted to hospitals, 12 were treated for gunshot wounds. In Nairobi, of the 125 who lost their lives, 23 died of gunshots while of the 342 admitted to hospitals, 61 had gunshot wounds.[91]

One can conclude that the police were trigger happy in areas they perceived as pro-ODM. Such attacks in pro-ODM zones were reinforced by a breakdown in the command chain within the force, with 'junior officers refus[ing] to take orders from their superiors' by 'placing ethnic loyalty before professional ethical conduct.'[92] In other cases, the command structure was abused from the top when high-ranking officers ordered their juniors to release people arrested for specific offences. Furthermore, the reported complacency within the force has been attributed to protests over the low pay for the extra-election work.

Police and Sexual Violence

By far the worst police atrocity was in relation to Sexual and Gender-Based Violence (SGBV). The CIPEV Report delves into the issue of SGBV in chapter six. It repeatedly refers to the role of the police who, at best, were indifferent to, or at worst were themselves perpetrators of the heinous crime. The indifference is best illustrated in the 'police commissioner [who] testified [to the Commission] that he could not determine whether sexual violence was fit to be reported...'[93] Not only did the police lack recorded reports of SGBV, they did not bother to proactively investigate it in the areas where evidence of it was likely to be found, for instance, Nairobi Women's Hospital.

The commissioner's response cited above fits into a pattern of indifference and denial regarding SGBV that started in Mt Elgon and culminated with PEV. Prior to the latter, instances of SGBV dotted the landscape, especially Mt Elgon district. In this region, the illegal Saboat Land Defence Force (SDLF) militia group had been terrorising citizens for awhile. The police belatedly responded with terror of their own. They isolated the men from the women and proceeded to subject the former to abuse while leaving the women extremely vulnerable. *Medecins Sans Frontieres*'s report of May 2008 gives heart-rending accounts of men whose testicles were pulled and who witnessed their wives being repeatedly raped by soldiers. For the women, there is a particularly disturbing report whose

91. CIPEV Report, pp. 392.
92. CIPEV Report, pp. 58, 128, 187. There is evidence of this in Naivasha and Homo Bay.
93. CIPEV Report, p. 257.

theme runs through many others about police methods. A woman in her late 20s recounts how soldiers walked into her house at night when her husband was away. They demanded to know why she was not pregnant and 'generously' offered, in her own words, to 'make me pregnant.' One soldier proceeded to forcibly pull down her pants and 'forced himself inside me' as the 'other soldier sat next to the bed watching the scene of action and next he took his turn and they went on and on.'[94]

The police commissioner has repeatedly denied these tales of deranged masculine sexual conquest and brutality, even though they are known to be in the arsenal of war. He may have assumed the women would remain silent, since sex is still taboo, with women fearing the public spectacle that often accompanies discussion of sexual abuse. But in the face of repeated public exposure as the excesses of Mt Elgon were taken up by human rights activists and the international community, police denials rang hollow. The climate of public awareness of SGBV came to colour much of the discussion of sexual abuse in PEV.

In the PEV, and notwithstanding the abundance of information, Major General Ali 'told the Commission the police had not collected any information or statistics on crime such as rapes.' This apparent lack of interest in sexual violence in general and particularly in not taking action against officers who perpetrated the crime is revealing about the masculinised ethos that dominates the force. Yet, it is clear that 'the involvement of state security agents in the perpetration of sexual violence and the fear of incriminating themselves may partly explain why the police omitted data on sexual violence in the reports they presented to the Commission.' The police, the CIPEV Report notes, exhibited 'a callous indifference if not outright hostility to victims who often experienced multiple tragedies ...'[95]

A total of 17 rapes during the course of PEV were committed by civilians and seven by police. Of the latter, 4 were committed by GSU, 2 by Administrative Police and 1 by Kenya Police. Samples of the testimonies collected by the Commission suffice to illustrate the abuse perpetrated by police or their indifference to reported cases. For instance, two victims, a 50-year-old widow and a 46-year-old married woman from the Kibera slums, were gang-raped by GSU personnel who entered their houses on the pretext of looking for weapons and the young men who were barricading roads and the railway line in Kibera.[96] A similar story is recounted by another 50-year-old woman from Kibera, who was raped along with her daughter at 6.30pm by GSU officers. This resulted in the

---

94. Medecins Sans Frontieres, *Does Anyone Care?* Medecins Sans Frontieres Report, May 2008, p. 9. http://www.msf.org/source/countries/africa/kenya/2008/MSF_MtElgon_May2008.pdf (browsed 21 April 2010).
95. CIPEV Report, p. 259.
96. CIPEV Report, p. 255.

daughter's falling pregnant, and a miscarriage in July 2008. In the Rift Valley town of Eldoret, the Commission heard a 17-year-old girl narrate how she was attacked by seven Administrative Police officers and gang-raped. This happened while she was running away from her sister's house, which was under attack by raiders.

Back in Nairobi, police responded with indifference to reports of rape. Cases are cited where police refused to record the evidence of sexual violence, demanded bribes in order to act or insisted that victims choose between rape and burglary in what they wished to report. Thus, a married woman in Mathare reported to the Pangani police station in Nairobi that she had been raped by people she knew very well. The police refused to take on the rape case, preferring that the woman reported robbery instead. After reporting the robbery, which was recorded in the Occurrence Book, those she identified were mysteriously released through political influence. A police officer from the station even demanded a bribe from the rape victim.[97]

The full gamut of these stories cannot be recounted here, but their implications for women are too obvious. Rape and sexual harassment remain a choice means of prosecuting war and Kenya's example illustrates how the breakdown of law and order opens the way for abuse.

---

97. CIPEV Report, p. 258.

Conclusion

Kenyan society was polarised prior to 2007. This polarisation has made having constructive debate on the origins and nature of post-election violence a difficult proposition. The polarisation follows the broad contours of the two top contending political parties, ODM and PNU. Those supporting the former tend to accept the view that PEV was due to election rigging that 'more or less invited popular rebellion against that unpopular and unjust abuse of the people's sovereignty.' Those favouring PNU perceive only murderous ethnic hatred in the actions of their opponent and paint Raila Odinga as ODM's anti-Gikuyu guardian. For them, PEV was 'forty-one tribes against one.' One would assume from these polar positions that PNU would support efforts to punish perpetrators of violence while ODM would be on the defensive, seeking to protect its luminaries from such punishment.

The post-election situation in Kenya has been a lot more complicated than the PNU/ODM outline assumes. While the PNU side was content to insist that ODM was guilty of ethnic cleansing and even genocide, they have not fully supported the desire of Kenyans to have the instigators of violence punished. On the ODM side, there has been a split in their ranks that threatens to fragment the party. Some members support punishment of the instigators of violence, coupled with their insistence that the original trigger of violence was election rigging, which in itself renders those who rigged the elections culpable.

The back and forth arguments on culpability have hardly helped the search for truth and justice. On the contrary, they have simply isolated the elite and exposed the central weakness that led to violence in the first place. By weakness, I refer to the breakdown of elite consensus prior to the elections regarding the importance and future of Kenya not only for Kenyans but also for elite interests. It may be presumptuous to suggest that the political class in Kenya has any national interests, given Makau Mutua's argument that they are beholden only to their personal interests and unable to imagine any national interest. However, we can at least concede that the elite recognises that its personal interests can only be served through an existing nation. It is the breakdown of an elite conversation regarding how their personal interests can be served through the nation that led them to mobilise their constituencies along ethnic lines and created the disaster that was PEV.

In other words, the general masses of Kenyans were pawns in an elite struggle for raw state power. Rather than using the experience of PEV to reform the state and politics, the post-election power-sharing arrangement brokered by Kofi Annan has become a negotiated elite pact, a pact that was postponed when NARC collapsed in 2005. But it has yet to deliver tangible benefits to the masses, except by returning temporary peace to the country. Most of the reform initiatives identified by the Kenya National Dialogue and Reconciliation have either become stalled or lag behind schedule. There have been repeated reminders that 'the window of opportunity to deliver reform is rapidly closing' and a candid admission from Kofi Annan that 'there is a crisis of confidence in Kenya's political leadership.'[98] However, the import of these reminders and admissions has hardly registered.

The challenge of PEV in Kenya is historical and stems from the fact that independent Kenya's leadership has never focused on the core task of nation-building. The leadership has sought legitimacy in authoritarianism rather than consent and has treated popular will with disdain. To paraphrase Claude Ake, the problem in Kenya is not so much that nation-building has failed but that it never began in the first place. The central preoccupation of leadership has been regime-building. These regimes have not only alienated significant segments of society, they have also been authoritarian and needed coercive structures and institutions to survive. These institutions and structures collapsed under the weight of internal suspicion and citizen anger during the PEV.

Susanne Mueller correctly observes that a diffusion of violence in society, coupled with the deliberate weakening of institutions of governance and ethnicisation of political parties, rendered the system vulnerable. However, the weakness in the internal working of the system was assisted by the deliberate weakening of the state in the context of external reform initiatives. State capacity to manage its affairs was weakened at the moment when it was required to open up to competitive politics. In other words, the state was required to deal with the heavy task of managing a serious transition at a time of greatest weakness. This weakness created more space for the insidious elite struggle to continue. What passes for competitive politics in Kenya is in fact an insidious struggle over raw power propelled by nothing more than the personalised interests of the elite.

In the pre-election period in Kenya, such competition became a zero-sum struggle. Groups of people were mobilised or willingly participated in what became a consuming competition that promised only one possible winner. Eventually, the side that mobilised a plurality of Kenyans 'lost.' The winner won by inflating vote tallies and rendering electoral choice useless.[99] There is also

---

98. Remarks by Kofi Annan on the conclusion of his visit to Kenya, 4–7 October 2009. See http://www.dialoguekenya.org/press.aspx, browsed on 10 February 2010.

99. This is according to the results of the only exit poll conducted by Clark C. Gibson and James D. Long. See their 'The Presidential and Parliamentary Elections in Kenya, December 2007,' in *Electoral Studies*, vol. 28, no. 3, 2009. The poll concluded that 'Taken together, Kibaki benefited from producing additional votes in seven provinces while losing votes in one; Odinga benefited from additional votes in one province and lost in seven. If we aggregate these net differences across provinces, we find that Kibaki benefited from 355,843 extra votes in the official tally when compared to the exit poll, while Odinga lost 57,951 votes, for a total of 413,794.' See p.500.

mounting evidence that the abuse of the electoral process was tacitly condoned, even approved, by Kenya's key partners, including the US, the UK and some UN institutions, like the World Bank. If PEV in Kenya has any lessons for further research work or the reform process, they are being lost with the focus on raw state power.

References

Abegaz, B., 2007, 'The 2005 Ethiopian Elections: Millstone or Milestone?', *Africa Review of Books*, vol. 3, no. 1.

Adejumobi, S., 2000, 'Elections in Africa: A Fading Shadow of Democracy,' *International Political Science Review*, vol. 21, no. 1.

Aina, T.A., 2008, 'The Kenyan Crisis 2007-2008 and the Re-Making of an Elite Consensus –Pathways and Pitfalls,' Lecture Delivered at the Public Forum organized by ARRF and DPMF held on Wednesday 3 September 2008 at the KICC, Nairobi.

Ake, C., 1996, *Democracy and Development in Africa*. Washington DC: Brookings Institution.

—, 1994, *Democratisation of Disempowerment in Africa*. CASS Occasional Monograph. Lagos: Malthouse.

Anderson, D., 2002, 'Vigilantes, Violence and the Politics of Public Order in Kenya,' *African Affairs*, vol. 101, no. 405.

—, (forthcoming), '*Majimboism*: The Troubled History of an Idea,' in D. Branch, N. Cheeseman and L. Gardner (eds), *Our Turn to Eat: Politics in Kenya since 1950*. Berlin: LIT Verlag.

Anderson, D. and E. Lochery, 2008, 'Violence and Exodus in Kenya's Rift Valley, 2008: Predictable and Preventable?' *Journal of Eastern African Studies*, vol. 2, no. 2.

Andreassen, B.A., et al., 2008, '*I Acted Under a Lot of Pressure': The Disputed 2007 Kenyan General Election in Context*. NORDEM Report, 7/2008.

Branch, D., 2009, *Defeating Mau Mau, Creating Kenya: Counterinsurgency, Civil War, and Decolonisation*. Cambridge: Cambridge University Press.

Branch, D., N. Cheeseman and L. Gardner (eds), 2010, *Our Turn to Eat: Politics in Kenya Since 1950*, Berlin: LIT Verlag.

Chabal, P. and J-P. Daloz, 1999, *Africa Works. The Political Instrumentalisation of Disorder*. Bloomington IN: International African Institute in association with James Currey and Indiana University Press.

Chege, M., 2009, 'Kenya: Back From the Brink?' *Journal of Democracy*, vol. 19, no. 4.

—, 2007, 'Weighed Down by Old Ethnic Baggage: Kenya Races to Another Historic Election,' at http://csis.org/blog/weighed-down-old-ethnic-baggage-kenya-races-another-historic-election posted on 22 June 2007, browsed on 19 October 2009.

Cheru, F., 1997, 'The Silent Revolution and the Weapons of the Weak: Transformation and Innovation from Below,' in Gill, S. and J. Mittelman (eds), *Innovation and Transformation in International Studies*. Cambridge: Cambridge University Press.

CIPEV, 2008, *Report of the Commission of Inquiry into Post Election Violence*. Nairobi: Government Printers.

Cottrell, J. and Y. Ghai, 2007, 'Constitution Making and Democratisation in Kenya (2000–05)', *Democratisation*, vol. 14, no. 1.

De Smedt, J., 2009, '"No Raila, No Peace!" Big Man Politics and Election Violence at the Kibera Grassroots,' *African Affairs*, vol. 108, no. 433.

Ellis, S., 1999, *The Mask of Anarchy: The Destruction of Liberia and the Religious Dimension of an African Civil War*. London: Hurst.

Fischer, J., 2002, *Electoral Conflict and Violence: A Strategy for Study and Prevention*, IFES White Paper, 2002-01, 5 February 2002.

Ghai, Y.P., 2008, 'Devolution: Restructuring the Kenyan State,' *Journal of Eastern African Studies*, vol. 2. no. 2.

Gibson, C.C. and J.D. Long, 2009, 'The Presidential and Parliamentary Elections in Kenya, December 2007,' *Electoral Studies*, vol. 28, no. 3.

Gimode, E., 2007, 'The Role of the Police in Kenya's Democratisation Process,' in Murunga, G.R. and S.W. Nasong'o (eds), *Kenya: Struggle for Democracy*. London and Dakar: Zed Books in association with CODESRIA.

Holmquist, F., 2005, 'Kenya's Antipolitics,' *Current History*, May 2005.

Human Rights Watch, 2008, *Ballots to Bullets Organized Political Violence and Kenya's Crisis of Governance*. HRW Report, vol. 20, no. 1, March 2008.

Ibrahim, J., 2007, *Nigeria's 2007 Elections: The Fitful Path to Democratic Citizenship*. Special Report no. 182, United States Institute of Peace.

Ihonvbere, J., 1996, 'Where is the Third Wave? A Critical Evaluation of Africa's Non-Transition to Democracy,' *Africa Today*, vol. 43, no. 4.

International Crisis Group, 2008, *Kenya in Crisis*, Africa Report no. 137, 21 February 2008.

IREC, 2008, *Report of the Independent Review Commission on the General Elections held in Kenya on the 27 December 2007*. Nairobi: Government Printers.

Kagwanja, P.M., 2008, 'Breaking Kenya's Impasse: Chaos or Courts?' *Africa Policy Brief*, no. 1.

—, 2006, '"Power to Uhuru": Youth Identity and Generational Politics in Kenya's 2002 Elections,' *Africa Affairs*, vol. 105, no. 418.

—, 2003, 'Facing Mount Kenya or Facing Mecca? The Mungiki, Ethnic Violence and the Politics of the Moi Succession in Kenya, 1987-2002,' *African Affairs*, vol. 102, no. 406.

Kalyvas, S., 2003, 'The Ontology of "Political Violence": Action and Identity in Civil Wars,' *Perspectives on Politics*, vol. 1, no. 3.

Karatnycky, A., 2005, 'Ukraine's Orange Revolution,' *Foreign Affairs*, vol. 84, no. 2.

Katumanga, M., 2005, 'A City under Siege: Banditry and Modes of Accumulation in Nairobi, 1991–2004,' *Review of African Political Economy*, no. 106.

Kimani, P., 2008, 'A Past of Power More than Tribe in Kenya's Turmoil,' http://www.opendemocracy.net/node/35486/pdf

Klopp, J. and P. Kamungi, 2007–08, 'Violence and Elections: Will Kenya Collapse?' *World Policy Journal*, vol. 24, no. 2, 2007–08.

KNCHR, 2008, *On The Brink of the Precipice: A Human Rights Account of Kenya's Post-2007 Election Violence*, 15 August 2008.

Lafargue, J. (ed.), 2009, *The General Elections in Kenya, 2007*. Dar es Salaam: Mkuki na Nyota.

Lynch, G., 2008, 'Courting the Kalenjin: The Failure of Dynasticism and the Strength of the ODM Wave in the Kenya's Rift Valley Province,' *African Affairs*, vol. 107, no. 429.

Manji, A., 2006, *The Politics of Land Reform in Africa: From Communal Tenure to Free Market*. London: Zed Books.

Maupeu, H., 2009, 'Revisiting Post-Election Violence,' in Lafargue, J. (ed.), *The General Elections in Kenya, 2007*. Dar es Salaam: Mkuki na Nyota.

Medecins Sans Frontieres, 2008, *Does Anyone Care?* Medecins Sans Frontieres Report, May 2008.

Mkandawire, T., 1999, 'Crisis Management and the Making of 'Choiceless Democracies' in Africa,' in Joseph, R. (ed.), *The State, Conflict and Democracy in Africa*. Boulder CO: Lynne Rienner.

Migai Akech, J.M., 2005, 'Public Law Values and the Politics of Criminal (In)justice: Creating a Democratic Framework for Policing in Kenya,' *Oxford University Commonwealth Law Journal*, vol. 5, no. 2.

Mkandawire, T. and C.C. Soludo, 1999, *Our Future, our Continent: African Perspectives on Structural Adjustment*. Ottawa and Dakar: IDRC and CODESRIA.

Mueller, S., 2008, 'The Political Economy of Kenya's Crisis,' *Journal of East African Studies*, vol. 2, no.2.

Murunga, G., 2007, 'Governance and the Politics of Structural Adjustment in Kenya,' in Murunga, G. and S. Nasong'o (eds), *Kenya: Struggles for Democracy*. London and Dakar: Zed Books in association with CODESRIA.

Murunga, G. and S.W. Nasong'o, 2006, 'Bent on Self-Destruction: The Kibaki Regime in Kenya', *Journal of Contemporary African Studies*, vol. 24, no. 1.

Mustapha, A.R. and L. Whitfield, 2009, *Turning Points in African Democracy*. London: James Currey.

Mutua, M., 2001, 'Justice under Siege: The Rule of Law and Judicial Subservience in Kenya,' *Human Rights Quarterly*, vol. 23, no. 1.

—, 2009, *Kenya's Quest for Democracy: Taming Leviathan*. Boulder and London: Lynne Rienner.

Mutunga, W., 1999, *Constitution Making from the Middle: Civil Society and Transition Politics in Kenya 1992-1997*. Nairobi: SAREAT.

Nasong'o, S.W., 2007, 'Negotiating New Rules of the Game: Social Movements, Civil Society and the Kenyan Transition,' in Murunga, G.R. and S.W. Nasong'o (eds), *Kenya: Struggle for Democracy*. London and Dakar: Zed Books in association with CODESRIA.

—, 2009, *The Human Rights Sector in Kenya: Key Issues and Challenges*. Occasional Paper No. 2. Nairobi: Kenya Human Rights Institute.

Ndegwa, S.N., 2003, 'Kenya: Third Time Lucky?' *Journal of Democracy*, vol. 14, no. 3.

N'Diaye, B., 2002, 'How Not to Institutionalize Civilian Control: Kenya's Coup Prevention Strategies, 1964–97,' *Armed Forces and Society*, vol. 24, no. 4.

Ngunyi, M., 2008, 'Civil Society in the Post-Amendment Context,' A Consultant's Report to the Royal Norwegian Embassy, Nairobi Kenya, June 2008.

—, 1996, 'Resuscitating the *Majimbo* Project: The Politics of Deconstructing the Unitary State in Kenya,' in Olukoshi A.O. and L. Laakso (eds), *Challenges to the Nation-State in Africa*. Uppsala: The Nordic Africa Institute.

Obi, C.I., 2008, *No Choice, But Democracy: Prising the People Out of Politics in Africa?* Claude Ake Memorial Paper No. 2, Department of Peace and Conflict Research, Uppsala University and Nordic Africa Institute.

—, 2008, 'International Election Observer Missions and the Promotion of Democracy: Some Lessons from Nigeria's 2007 Elections,' *Politikon*, vol. 35, no. 1.

Olukoshi, A.O., *The Elusive Prince of Denmark: Structural Adjustment and the Crisis of Governance in Africa*. Research Report No. 104. Uppsala: The Nordic Africa Institute.

—, 2005, 'Changing Patterns of Politics in Africa,' in Boron, A.A. and G. Lechini (eds), *Politics and Social Movements in an Hegemonic World: Lessons from Africa, Asia and Latin America*. Buenos Aires: CLACSO.

Omotola, J.S., 2009, '"Garrison" Democracy in Nigeria: The 2007 General Elections and the Prospects of Democratic Consolidation,' *Commonwealth and Comparative Politics*, vol. 47, no. 2.

Ong'wen, O., 2008, 'Class vs Kinship in Kenya's Eruption to Violence,' *Wajibu*, vol. 23, no. 1.

Onoma, A.K., 2010, *The Politics of Property Rights Institutions in Africa*. Cambridge: Cambridge University Press.

Otieno, G., 2005, 'The NARC's Anti-Corruption Drive: Somewhere Over the Rainbow?' *Africa Security Review*, vol. 14, no. 4.

Owour, Y.A., 2009, 'Contemporary Projections: Africa in the Literature of Atrocity (Aftrocity),' in Ndibe, O. and C. Hove (eds), *Writers, Writing on Conflicts and Wars in Africa*. London and Uppsala: Adonis and Abbey Publishers and Nordic Africa Institute.

Shivji, I.G., 2009, *Where is Uhuru? Reflections on the Struggle for Democracy in Africa*. Oxford: Fahamu Books.

—, 1990, 'The Pitfalls in the Debate on Democracy,' *CODESRIA Bulletin*, no. 1.

Smith, L., 2009, 'Explaining Violence after Recent Elections in Ethiopia and Kenya,' *Democratization*, vol. 16, no. 5.

Society for International Development (SID), 2006, *Readings on Inequality in Kenya: Sectoral Dynamics and Perspectives*. Nairobi: SID.

Tamarkin, M., 1978, 'The Roots of Political Stability in Kenya,' *African Affairs*, vol. 77, no. 308.

Tostensen, A., 2009, 'Electoral Mismanagement and Post-Election Violence in Kenya: The Kriengler and Waki Commissions of Inquiry,' *Nordic Journal of Human Rights/ Nordisk Tidsskrift for Menneskerettigheter,* vol. 27, no. 4.

Wainaina, B., 2008, 'In Gikuyu, for Gikuyu, of Gikuyu,' *Granta* 103, Autumn 2008 http://www.granta.com/Magazine/Granta-103/Letter-From/1

Wamue, G.N., 2001, 'Revisiting Our Indigenous Shrines through Mungiki,' *African Affairs*, vol. 100, no. 400.

Wrong, M., 2009, *It's Our Time to Eat: The Story of a Kenyan Whistle Blower*. London: Fourth Estate.

DISCUSSION PAPERS PUBLISHED BY THE INSTITUTE

Recent issues in the series are available electronically for download free of charge
www.nai.uu.se

1. Kenneth Hermele and Bertil Odén, *Sanctions and Dilemmas. Some Implications of Economic Sanctions against South Africa.*
1988. 43 pp. ISBN 91-7106-286-6

2. Elling Njål Tjønneland, *Pax Pretoriana. The Fall of Apartheid and the Politics of Regional Destabilisation.*
1989. 31 pp. ISBN 91-7106-292-0

3. Hans Gustafsson, Bertil Odén and Andreas Tegen, *South African Minerals. An Analysis of Western Dependence.*
1990. 47 pp. ISBN 91-7106-307-2

4. Bertil Egerö, *South African Bantustans. From Dumping Grounds to Battlefronts.*
1991. 46 pp. ISBN 91-7106-315-3

5. Carlos Lopes, *Enough is Enough! For an Alternative Diagnosis of the African Crisis.*
1994. 38 pp. ISBN 91-7106-347-1

6. Annika Dahlberg, *Contesting Views and Changing Paradigms.*
1994. 59 pp. ISBN 91-7106-357-9

7. Bertil Odén, *Southern African Futures. Critical Factors for Regional Development in Southern Africa.*
1996. 35 pp. ISBN 91-7106-392-7

8. Colin Leys and Mahmood Mamdani, *Crisis and Reconstruction – African Perspectives.*
1997. 26 pp. ISBN 91-7106-417-6

9. Gudrun Dahl, *Responsibility and Partnership in Swedish Aid Discourse.*
2001. 30 pp. ISBN 91-7106-473-7

10. Henning Melber and Christopher Saunders, *Transition in Southern Africa – Comparative Aspects.*
2001. 28 pp. ISBN 91-7106-480-X

11. *Regionalism and Regional Integration in Africa.*
2001. 74 pp. ISBN 91-7106-484-2

12. Souleymane Bachir Diagne, et al., *Identity and Beyond: Rethinking Africanity.*
2001. 33 pp. ISBN 91-7106-487-7

13. Georges Nzongola-Ntalaja, et al., *Africa in the New Millennium.* Edited by Raymond Suttner.
2001. 53 pp. ISBN 91-7106-488-5

14. *Zimbabwe's Presidential Elections 2002.* Edited by Henning Melber.
2002. 88 pp. ISBN 91-7106-490-7

15. Birgit Brock-Utne, *Language, Education and Democracy in Africa.*
2002. 47 pp. ISBN 91-7106-491-5

16. Henning Melber et al., *The New Partnership for Africa's development (NEPAD).*
2002. 36 pp. ISBN 91-7106-492-3

17. Juma Okuku, *Ethnicity, State Power and the Democratisation Process in Uganda.*
2002. 42 pp. ISBN 91-7106-493-1

18. Yul Derek Davids, et al., *Measuring Democracy and Human Rights in Southern Africa.* Compiled by Henning Melber.
2002. 50 pp. ISBN 91-7106-497-4

19. Michael Neocosmos, Raymond Suttner and Ian Taylor, *Political Cultures in Democratic South Africa.* Compiled by Henning Melber.
2002. 52 pp. ISBN 91-7106-498-2

20. Martin Legassick, *Armed Struggle and Democracy. The Case of South Africa.*
2002. 53 pp. ISBN 91-7106-504-0

21. Reinhart Kössler, Henning Melber and Per Strand, *Development from Below. A Namibian Case Study.*
2003. 32 pp. ISBN 91-7106-507-5

22. Fred Hendricks, *Fault-Lines in South African Democracy. Continuing Crises of Inequality and Injustice.*
2003. 32 pp. ISBN 91-7106-508-3

23. Kenneth Good, *Bushmen and Diamonds. (Un) Civil Society in Botswana.*
2003. 39 pp. ISBN 91-7106-520-2

24. Robert Kappel, Andreas Mehler, Henning Melber and Anders Danielson, *Structural Stability in an African Context.*
2003. 55 pp. ISBN 91-7106-521-0

25. Patrick Bond, *South Africa and Global Apartheid. Continental and International Policies and Politics.*
2004. 45 pp. ISBN 91-7106-523-7

26. Bonnie Campbell (ed.), *Regulating Mining in Africa. For whose benefit?*
2004. 89 pp. ISBN 91-7106-527-X

27. Suzanne Dansereau and Mario Zamponi, *Zimbabwe – The Political Economy of Decline.* Compiled by Henning Melber.
2005. 43 pp. ISBN 91-7106-541-5

28. Lars Buur and Helene Maria Kyed, *State Recognition of Traditional Authority in Mozambique. The nexus of Community Representation and State Assist-ance.*
2005. 30 pp. ISBN 91-7106-547-4

29. Hans Eriksson and Björn Hagströmer, *Chad – Towards Democratisation or Petro-Dictatorship?*
2005. 82 pp.ISBN 91-7106-549-

30. Mai Palmberg and Ranka Primorac (eds), *Skinning the Skunk – Facing Zimbabwean Futures.*
2005. 40 pp. ISBN 91-7106-552-0

31. Michael Brüntrup, Henning Melber and Ian Taylor, *Africa, Regional Cooperation and the World Market – Socio-Economic Strategies in Times of Global Trade Regimes.* Com-piled by Henning Melber.
2006. 70 pp. ISBN 91-7106-559-8

32. Fibian Kavulani Lukalo, *Extended Handshake or Wrestling Match? – Youth and Urban Culture Celebrating Politics in Kenya.*
2006.58 pp. ISBN 91-7106-567-9

33. Tekeste Negash, *Education in Ethiopia: From Crisis to the Brink of Collapse.*
2006. 55 pp. ISBN 91-7106-576-8

34. Fredrik Söderbaum and Ian Taylor (eds) *Micro-Regionalism in West Africa. Evidence from Two Case Studies.*
2006. 32 pp. ISBN 91-7106-584-9

35. Henning Melber (ed.), *On Africa – Scholars and African Studies.*
2006. 68 pp. ISBN 978-91-7106-585-8

36. Amadu Sesay, *Does One Size Fit All? The Sierra Leone Truth and Reconciliation Commission Revisited.*
2007. 56 pp. ISBN 978-91-7106-586-5

37. Karolina Hulterström, Amin Y. Kamete and Henning Melber, *Political Opposition in African Countries – The Case of Kenya, Namibia, Zambia and Zimbabwe.*
2007. 86 pp. ISBN 978-7106-587-2

38. Henning Melber (ed.), *Governance and State Delivery in Southern Africa. Examples from Botswana, Namibia and Zimbabwe.*
2007. 65 pp. ISBN 978-91-7106-587-2

39. Cyril Obi (ed.), *Perspectives on Côte d'Ivoire: Between Political Breakdown and Post-Conflict Peace.*
2007. 66 pp. ISBN 978-91-7106-606-6

40. Anna Chitando, *Imagining a Peaceful Society. A Vision of Children's Literature in a Post-Conflict Zimbabwe.*
2008. 26 pp. ISBN 978-91-7106-623-7

41. Olawale Ismail, *The Dynamics of Post-Conflict Reconstruction and Peace Building in West Africa. Between Change and Stability.*
2009.52 pp. ISBN 978-91-7106-637-4

42. Ron Sandrey and Hannah Edinger, *Examining the South Africa–China Agricultural Relationship.*
2009. 58 pp. ISBN 978-91-7106-643-5

43. Xuan Gao, *The Proliferation of Anti-Dumping and Poor Governance in Emerging Economies.*
2009. 41 pp. ISBN 978-91-7106-644-2

44. Lawal Mohammed Marafa, *Africa's Business and Development Relationship with China. Seeking Moral and Capital Values of the Last Economic Frontier.*
2009. xx pp. ISBN 978-91-7106-645-9

45. Mwangi wa Githinji, *Is That a Dragon or an Elephant on Your Ladder? The Potential Impact of China and India on Export Led Growth in African Countries.*
2009. 40 pp. ISBN 978-91-7106-646-6

46. Jo-Ansie van Wyk, *Cadres, Capitalists, Elites and Coalitions. The ANC, Business and Development in South Africa.*
2009. 61 pp. ISBN 978-91-7106-656-5

47. Elias Courson, *Movement for the Emancipation of the Niger Delta (MEND). Political Marginalization, Repression and Petro-Insurgency in the Niger Delta.*2009. 30 pp. ISBN 978-91-7106-657-2

48. Babatunde Ahonsi, *Gender Violence and HIV/AIDS in Post-Conflict West Africa. Issues and Responses.* 2010.
38 pp. ISBN 978-91-7106-665-7

49. Usman Tar and Abba Gana Shettima, *Endangered Democracy? The Struggle over Secularism and its Implications for Politics and Democracy in Nigeria.*
2010. 21 pp. ISBN 978-91-7106-666-4

50. Garth Andrew Myers, *Seven Themes in African Urban Dynamics.*2010. 28 pp.
ISBN 978-91-7106-677-0

51. Abdoumaliq Simone, *The Social Infrastructures of City Life in Contemporary Africa.*
2010. 33 pp. ISBN 978-91-7106-678-7

52. Li Anshan, *Chinese Medical Cooperation in Africa. With Special Emphasis on the Medical Teams and Anti-Malaria Campaign.*
2011. 24 pp. ISBN 978-91-7106-683-1

53. Folashade Hunsu, *Zangbeto: Navigating the Spaces Between Oral art, Communal Security And Conflict Mediation in Badagry, Nigeria.*
2011. 27 pp. ISBN 978-91-7106-688-6

54. Jeremiah O. Arowosegbe, *Reflections on the Challenge of Reconstructing Post-Conflict States in West Africa: Insights from Claude Ake's Political Writings.*
2011. 40 pp. ISBN 978-91-7106-689-3

55. Bertil Odén, *The Africa Policies of Nordic Countries and the Erosion of the Nordic Aid Model: A comparative study.*
2011. 66 pp. ISBN 978-91-7106-691-6

56. Angela Meyer, *Peace and Security Cooperation in Central Africa: Developments, Challenges and Prospects.*
2011. 47 pp ISBN 978-91-7106-693-0

57. Godwin R. Murunga, *Spontaneous or Premeditated? Post-Election Violence in Kenya.*
2011. 58 pp. ISBN 978-91-7106-694-7